SOLVING CRIMES WITH PHYSICS

FORENSICS:
THE SCIENCE OF CRIME-SOLVING

TITLE LIST

Computer Investigation

Criminal Psychology and Personality Profiling

DNA Analysis

Document Analysis

Entomology and Palynology: Evidence from the Natural World

Explosives and Arson Investigation

Fingerprints, Bite Marks, Ear Prints: Human Signposts

Forensic Anthropology

Forensics in American Culture: Obsessed with Crime

Mark and Trace Analysis

Pathology

Solving Crimes with Physics

SOLVING CRIMES WITH PHYSICS

by William Hunter

Mason Crest Publishers
Philadelphia

Mason Crest Publishers Inc.
370 Reed Road
Broomall, Pennsylvania 19008
(866) MCP-BOOK (toll free)

First printing
1 2 3 4 5 6 7 8 9 10

Library of Congress Cataloging-in-Publication Data

Hunter, William, 1971–
  Solving crimes with physics / by William Hunter.
      p. cm. — (Forensics, the science of crime-solving)
  Includes bibliographical references and index.
  ISBN 1-4222-0036-1   ISBN 1-4222-0025-6 (series)
  1. Forensic sciences. 2. Criminal investigation. I. Title. II.
Series.
  HV8073.H894 2006
  363.25—dc22
                                                    2005018616

Produced by Harding House Publishing Service, Inc.
www.hardinghousepages.com
Interior and cover design by MK Bassett-Harvey.
Printed in India.

Contents

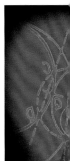

Introduction

By Jay A. Siegel, Ph.D.
Director, Forensic and Investigative Sciences Program
Indiana University, Purdue University, Indianapolis

It seems like every day the news brings forth another story about crime in the United States. Although the crime rate has been slowly decreasing over the past few years (due perhaps in part to the aging of the population), crime continues to be a very serious problem. Increasingly, the stories we read that involve crimes also mention the role that forensic science plays in solving serious crimes. Sensational crimes such as the O. J. Simpson case, or more recently, the Laci Peterson tragedy, provide real examples of the power of forensic science. In recent years there has been an explosion of books, movies, and TV shows devoted to forensic science and crime investigation. The wondrously successful *CSI* TV shows have spawned a major increase in awareness of and interest in forensic science as a tool for solving crimes. *CSI* even has its own syndrome: the "*CSI* Effect," wherein jurors in real cases expect to hear testimony about science such as fingerprints, DNA, and blood spatter because they saw it on TV.

The unprecedented rise in the public's interest in forensic science has fueled demands by students and parents for more educational programs that teach the applications of science to crime. This started in colleges and universities but has filtered down to high schools and middle schools. Even elementary school students now learn how science is used in the criminal justice system. Most educators agree that this developing interest in forensic science is a good thing. It has provided an excellent opportunity to teach students science—and they have fun learning it! Forensic science is an ideal vehicle for teaching science for several reasons. It is truly multidisciplinary;

practically every field of science has forensic applications. Successful forensic scientists must be good problem solvers and critical thinkers. These are critical skills that all students need to develop.

In all of this rush to implement forensic science courses in secondary schools throughout North America, the development of grade-appropriate resources that help guide students and teachers is seriously lacking. There are very few college and high school textbooks and none that are appropriate for younger students. That is why this new series: FORENSICS: THE SCIENCE OF CRIME-SOLVING is so important and so timely. Each book in the series contains a concise, age-appropriate discussion of one or more areas of forensic science.

Students are never too young to begin to learn the principles and applications of science. Forensic science provides an interesting and informative way to introduce scientific concepts in a way that grabs and holds the students' attention. FORENSICS: THE SCIENCE OF CRIME-SOLVING promises to be an important resource in teaching forensic science to students twelve to eighteen years old.

CHAPTER ONE

Introducing Forensic Science

In November 1963, President John F. Kennedy decided to visit Dallas, Texas, for a variety of political reasons. When he announced his decision, the Secret Service had some concerns about security, since UN Ambassador Adlai Stevenson had been jeered, jostled, struck by a protest sign, and spat upon in a visit to Dallas the previous month. To prevent a similar incident, Dallas police prepared the most stringent security precautions in the city's history.

Kennedy would travel from the Love Field airport in a motorcade through downtown Dallas to give a speech at the Dallas Trade Mart in suburban Dallas. The car in which he was traveling was an open-top limousine, which would allow crowds to see Kennedy as he traveled. (No presidential car with a bullet-proof top was yet in service in 1963.) Riding with Kennedy in the limousine were his wife, Texas governor John Connally Sr., Connally's wife, and two Secret Service agents.

The presidential motorcade traveled nearly its entire route without incident, stopping twice so Kennedy could shake hands with some Catholic nuns, then some schoolchildren. And then, shortly after noon, the nation's worst nightmare became a reality.

As the limousine passed through the crowds, Kennedy was shot at for an estimated six to nine seconds. During the shooting, the limousine is calculated to have slowed from over 13 miles per hour to only 9 miles per hour. The *Warren Commission* later concluded that one of the three shots likely missed the motorcade, that the first bullet to hit anyone went straight through Kennedy and likely also caused all of Connally's injuries, and the last bullet to hit anyone opened a fatal wound in Kennedy's head. Most investigators agree that Kennedy was hit with at least two bullets, and that he was killed when shot in the head. (However, another popular theory deals with the idea that only one bullet hit Kennedy: the Magic Bullet Theory.)

President John F. Kennedy (left) during an earlier motorcade.

The crowd barely reacted to the first shot; later, many witnesses said they thought they had heard a firecracker or a car backfire. Only after Governor Connally was injured and had screamed, "No, no, no. They are going to kill us all!" did the situation become clear to the Secret Service limousine driver, Bill Greer.

Investigators have determined that when Kennedy's head was struck, it moved slightly forward and down one to two inches (25 to 50 millimeters). The cause of what happened next is an issue that has kept people investigating the assassination. As the wound to the right side of his skull opened up, the president's right shoulder twisted forward and slightly upward, then his torso moved quickly backward and to the left before he bounced off the rear seat vertical cushion and slumped left toward his wife. When Mr. Greer realized the president had been wounded, the limousine sped up and proceeded to the hospital. A shocked nation would hear the news an hour later: the president was dead.

In the years since Kennedy's assassination, there has been an ongoing debate about the physics of the fatal shot that struck President Kennedy in the head. These questions have led to the suspicion that unknown agents might have been involved with the assassination (besides Lee Harvey Oswald, who was arrested for the crime). Although there is very strong evidence that the fatal shot came from the right rear (where the sixth-floor sniper's nest in the Texas School Book Depository was located), JFK's head and body moved backward and to the left with significant speed immediately after the head shot. Conspiracy theorists point to this rearward kick of the body as evidence of a shot from the grassy knoll located ahead and to the right of the president.

Clearly, matter exited the president's head with significant speed. Analysis by physics experts shows that the forward ejection of matter from the head can carry more rearward momentum than the incoming bullet possessed, due to the sudden release of pressure built up in the skull as the bullet passed through, as was discussed in a 1976 *Physics Today* article by Nobel physicist Luis Alvarez. Other experts in physics conclude that conspiracy theories are not necessary to explain Kennedy's murder.

A BRIEF INTRODUCTION TO FORENSIC SCIENCE

Obviously, not all crimes are as high profile as President Kennedy's assassination. Not every crime shakes an entire nation the way this one did—but all crimes shake the worlds of those who are touched by them.

No one wants to become a victim, nor do we want our families or friends to be victimized. We are all interested in preventing crimes or solving them. Forensic science is a field where law and science intersect. Highly trained experts examine evidence collected from a crime scene and look for ways to connect an individual to that particular crime. The connections can number in the hundreds in some cases. In other cases there is only a handful to be found. Each case is different, as is each crime scene. A forensic scientist knows the tricks of the trade to find the connections between a crime and the criminal. Many kinds of science can be involved with forensics—including physics.

Every society in the world is governed by some kind of laws. These laws vary from place to place, but all are made to protect the integrity of the society. They are not all the same, because each society has different traditions to protect, but nearly every law is designed to protect the rights of law-abiding people from less scrupulous individuals found around the world. There are always people willing to ignore the rights of others to get something they want.

Since the beginning of recorded history, there have been references to crime and punishment. For many centuries, fighting crime was largely based on word of mouth and eyewitness accounts. The only way to solve a crime in the first few thousand years of written history was to find a person who saw the suspect committing the crime. Other types of evidence were unheard of. Without an eyewitness, most crimes went un-solved.

As people learned more about the world around them, the different sciences were developed. Biology, chemistry, and physics are each the sum of thousands of independent discoveries by people over the years. The nature of science is that each discovery opens the door for further discovery. As science has advanced, technology has also moved forward. Technological advances, in turn, are the driving force behind the great leaps in science over the past century.

Science has made many advances in recent years.

There are few areas of science that operate under the lens of public awareness like forensic science. The development of such popular television shows as CSI, in all of its different forms, is one way that forensic science has been thrust into the public eye.

Interestingly, as the number of television shows using forensic analysis to drive the plot has grown, so has the demand for more forensic science training programs. It is probably wrong to assume that the growth in forensic science is solely attributable to pop culture, but most experts agree the explosion in popularity of these television shows has had an effect on the level of interest around the country, and this has been good for crime fighting.

As technology advanced, it became increasingly clear that science could help solve crimes. The development of modern-day forensic science began slowly but gained momentum with the invention of tools like the microscope. Clues left behind during a crime are often so small they cannot be seen by the naked eye, but with the use of microscopes, they can prove useful to investigators. The powerful computers that are commercially available have also provided a huge boost to the development of crime-fighting techniques.

Over the years, forensic science has evolved into a vast and powerful crime-solving tool, enabling investigators to catch criminals who would have gone free just fifty years ago. Technology used by forensic experts is often at the cutting edge of science. When a case is as famous and controversial as

New technologies allow forensic scientists to solve crimes faster.

Kennedy's assassination, scientists will likely be applying new technology to past events for years to come.

KEY CONCEPTS OF FORENSIC SCIENCE

Criminals often think they have committed the "perfect crime." They work hard to clean up after themselves and are extremely careful not to leave any visible sign of their presence. What most criminals do not realize, however, is that there is always evidence left behind. The basic concept behind all of forensic science is the Principle of Exchange, put forward in 1910 by a criminologist named Edmund Locard. This theory holds that every time a person touches something, he leaves

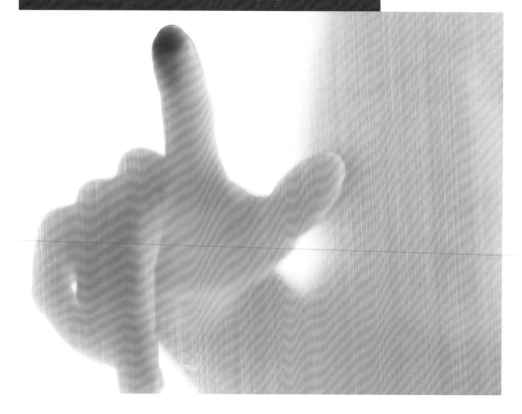

Whenever we touch something, an exchange of matter occurs.

Ancient Forensics

The first written method including forensic applications came from ancient China, where a doctor noted it was possible to tell if a person found dead in a pond had died from drowning or had been dead before being placed in the water. The ability to determine whether a person died in the water does not provide clues as to the identity of the killer, but it does indicate whether the death may have involved foul play. Dead people do not tend to move around much on their own, do they? Someone had to put the body into the water.

behind a physical trace of that contact. It may be amazingly small, but the trace is always there. Knowing where to look and how to collect the evidence is the specialty of a forensic scientist. The Principle of Exchange is perhaps the most critical theory in forensic science and is the driving force behind most criminal investigations.

In addition to the Principle of Exchange, the basic theories of science are important to solving many forensic cases. Forensic biologists, who use their knowledge of biological systems and patterns to provide information about the identity of a criminal, rely heavily on the basic concepts of *genetics*. Forensic *entomologists* use their knowledge of the development of insects to help estimate the amount of time a body has

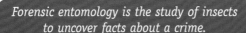

Forensic entomology is the study of insects to uncover facts about a crime.

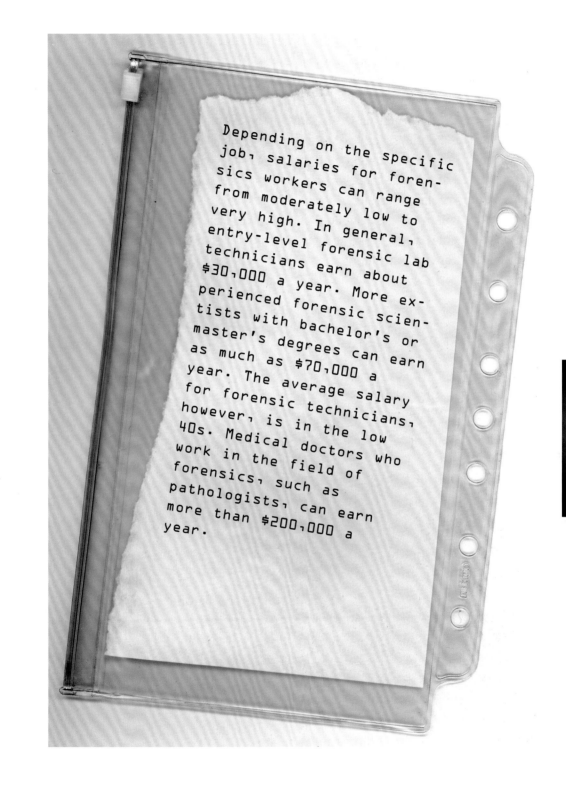

Depending on the specific job, salaries for forensics workers can range from moderately low to very high. In general, entry-level forensic lab technicians earn about $30,000 a year. More experienced forensic scientists with bachelor's or master's degrees can earn as much as $70,000 a year. The average salary for forensic technicians, however, is in the low 40s. Medical doctors who work in the field of forensics, such as pathologists, can earn more than $200,000 a year.

been decaying and, therefore, the time of death. The development of DNA profiling and many other powerful forensic techniques are based on years of scientific research using the theories of biological science.

A sound understanding of the nature of chemistry can be vital to gathering as much information as possible. When traces of chemicals are found at a crime scene, it is the job of a forensic chemist to figure out what they are. Usually, a few standard chemical tests can reveal the identity of these compounds. Many of the techniques used in forensic laboratories rely on the scientist having at least a basic understanding of the theories of chemistry.

Chemistry reveals the identities of foreign substances.

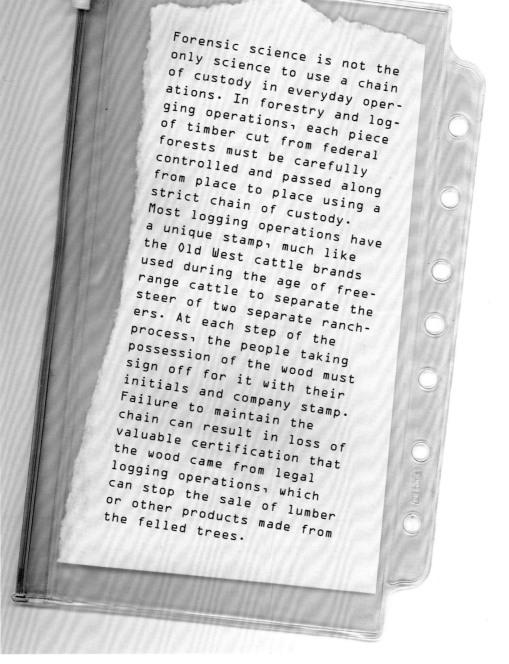

Forensic science is not the only science to use a chain of custody in everyday operations. In forestry and logging operations, each piece of timber cut from federal forests must be carefully controlled and passed along from place to place using a strict chain of custody. Most logging operations have a unique stamp, much like the Old West cattle brands used during the age of free-range cattle to separate the steer of two separate ranchers. At each step of the process, the people taking possession of the wood must sign off for it with their initials and company stamp. Failure to maintain the chain can result in loss of valuable certification that the wood came from legal logging operations, which can stop the sale of lumber or other products made from the felled trees.

The theories of physics are often important in the recon-struction of a crime scene. Theories of motion and energy are critical parts of the physicist's bag of tricks that can be useful in a forensic setting. Nearly every crime involves something in motion; it is the job of the physicist to analyze that evidence.

CRIME SCENES AND THE ROLE OF FORENSIC SCIENTISTS

While popular media often portrays the forensic scientist as a jack-of-all-trades who goes out to crime scenes and processes all manner of evidence, the truth is that most forensic scien-tists are specialists in relatively narrow disciplines of forensic science. For example, a forensic biologist works mainly with blood evidence, developing DNA profiles and providing informa-tion about the types of proteins found in the blood. Most of a forensic scientist's work is done in a very specialized laboratory designed to process the specific evidence type they must exam-ine.

Most forensic experts never get anywhere near an actual crime scene unless they are involved in a crime themselves. Specialists who are part of a team called the evidence collec-tion unit (ECU), deal with crime-scene examination. Individuals working in the ECU do not do much in the crime laboratory; their responsibility is to find and collect crime-scene evidence. The ECU must treat each crime scene individu-ally because no two scenes are alike, and evidence can be hidden in the unlikeliest of places. Training to become an ev-idence collector occurs mostly on the job, working closely with an experienced collector.

At most crime scenes, the first step is to secure the evi-dence by preventing people from trampling it. Normally the first-responders to the scene, the police, handle this. The ECU is responsible for carefully and methodically analyzing the crime scene, looking for as much evidence as possible. Typically, the scene will be divided into a grid—the most effi-cient and thorough method for finding evidence. Once the grid

Photographs are taken to document the crime scene.

Evidence is processed in the lab, not at the crime scene.

is established, the crime scene is sketched and photographed so each piece of evidence that is collected can be linked to its proper location at the scene. These photographs often serve as evidence themselves. As evidence is collected, it is bagged, tagged, and labeled with the proper grid location. One of the most critical steps in evidence collection is the "chain of custody." Every piece of evidence must be handled in accordance with the rules of the chain of custody, which require that each person who handles the evidence signs for it before he can take possession of it. A break in the chain of custody can be enough for a judge to disallow the use of a piece of evidence in a trial—something for which no forensics expert wants to be responsible.

Collected evidence is cataloged and sent to the proper department at the crime laboratory for processing. Specialists who work only with particular evidence types staff each department. Each evidence type has its own specialized department in order to reduce errors and obtain the maximum amount of information each bit can provide. The evidence is examined exhaustively as every single bit of information can be crucial to the case at hand. One mistake can be enough to allow a criminal to walk free. Because of the importance of their work, forensic experts are required to train long hours in the laboratory before they are allowed to work alone.

When physics is applied to forensics, experts will rely on various types of physical evidence—such as blood *spatter*, bullets, and wounds—as well as accounts of events from eyewitnesses. Experts can then piece together these facts to form a better picture of how a crime was committed—and who did it.

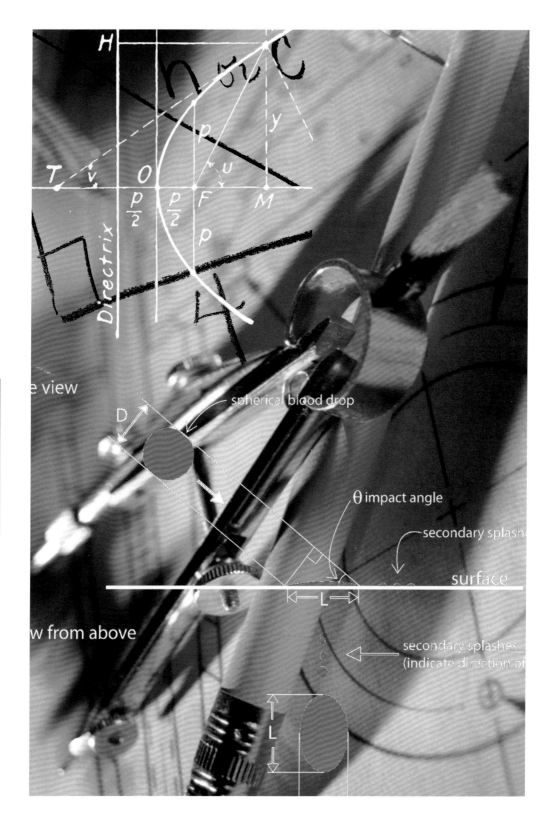

e view

spherical blood drop

D

θ impact angle

secondary splash

surface

L

w from above

secondary splashes
(indicate direction of

CHAPTER TWO

Introducing Physics

On September 4, 1998, Carl Gustafson was walking home from a tavern with a friend. The path they chose took them past a neighborhood party. As they passed the house where the party was taking place, a man named Jeremy Bell came out and assaulted Gustafson. Other partygoers and Gustafson's friend helped separate the two, and Gustafson, saying he did not want any trouble, walked off with his friend.

A short while later, a man identified as someone other than Gustafson confronted the partygoers with a loaded shotgun, asking why they had assaulted Gustafson. When Bell, who had left the party, heard about the episode with the man holding the shotgun, he turned around and made his way back toward the party. About the same time, Gustafson returned to the area looking for his eyeglasses, which had been knocked off during the scuffle. Bell saw him walking near the house where the party was held, and stooped to pick up a baseball bat he found in a nearby yard.

As Gustafson searched for his glasses, Bell came up behind him and struck him—hard—to the head. Witnesses reported hearing a cracking noise as the blow fell. Gustafson immediately collapsed to the ground, where he lay until a few party-goers and Bell took him to the hospital emergency room. Gustafson died ten days later from the massive head trauma he suffered that night.

A jury deemed the violent blow Bell delivered to Gustafson's head to be excessive force, and convicted Bell of second-degree murder. Bell argued that he was defending himself and his friends from Gustafson, whom he said he thought was holding a gun. Forensic analysis of the wound and blood spatter, however, proved to be important evidence that indicated the blow was the result of a vicious attack, clearly meant to harm the victim. Physics proved that Bell was lying.

Forensic analysis reveals the true nature of a person's death.

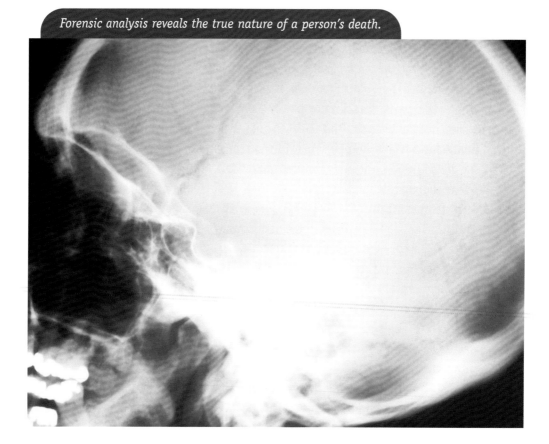

The force of gravity is a basic aspect of physics. Scientific tests of the effects of gravity have long proven that the acceleration of an object falling through the atmosphere is about thirty-two feet (9.8 meters) per second. Newton believed gravity worked because every object has a degree of attractive force on every object around it. The more massive the object is, the greater the force of the attraction. The Earth, being the most massive object around, exerts a very strong force on the objects that sit on its surface. Astronomers believe the force of gravity on other planets can be calculated by comparing the size of those planets to the Earth. We can see from watching the leaping antics of humans on the moon that a gravitational force draws the people back to the surface, or else when they jumped they would have flown off into space, never to be seen again.

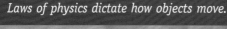

Think about this for a moment: a tennis ball dropped from the top of New York City's Empire State Building, which stands 1,453 feet (443 meters) high, falls for about 9.5 seconds before it hits the ground. At the moment it hits the ground, the ball will be moving along at about 305 feet (93 meters) each second, or approximately 208 mph! Why is the ball moving so fast? Most people quickly answer: gravity. But what is gravity, and how can we predict the speed the ball will reach during the fall? The answer is simple: we use our knowledge of physics.

Every single day people use a basic understanding of this science to move about and avoid being hit by other moving

Laws of physics dictate how objects move.

Physics at the Movies

The laser cannons in <u>Star Wars</u>—supposedly focused beams of light—would move through space so fast there would be no way a person's eye could detect their motion at close range, unless the beam was left on for a long period of time and fired through a cloud of dust. Of course, the visual effect is important to the success of the movie, so go ahead and suspend reality for the films.

things. A good illustration of this is the game of dodge ball. A thrown ball moves so predictably that a person can either dodge the throw or step into the ball's path and try to catch it. We know the ball is not going to suddenly change direction in mid-flight; thrown objects simply do not act that way. Imagine the game of baseball if this were not the case! Many more people would be hit by pitches if the ball randomly changed direction. The same principle is true of falling things—they tend to fall straight to the ground as gravity acts on them, gaining speed as they go (rather than shooting off to one side or the other). It has always been this way because physics is part of the natural world.

Air resistance is such a powerful force on a moving object that it can actually affect the distance something travels, even if the distance is very short. Take, for example, the motion of a baseball through air after being hit by a bat. A baseball that would fly 400 feet (122 meters) at sea level with no wind would fly farther at higher altitudes because it would be affected by factors such as altitude, temperature, and relative humidity. Why? At higher altitudes, the air itself is under less pressure, meaning the molecules are more spread out than at lower altitudes. Molecules of air at higher temperatures are also more spread out because the heat energy that changes the air temperature affects the molecules, and they move apart from one another. Relative humidity matters because it is a measure of the number of water droplets in the air in any one location; try throwing a ball through water sometime. The effect of increasing altitude is an increase in ball flight of about six feet (1.8 meters) in extra distance for every 1,000 feet (305 meters) of additional altitude. Similarly, an increase in temperature of only ten degrees can add four feet (1.2 meters) to a ball's flight.

THE SCIENCE OF MOTION

Look around. Everywhere you look things are in motion. Pay attention to the way the objects move, and you will notice these motions are usually predictable. This fact is true everywhere in the world. Sir Isaac Newton noticed it and authored his famous Laws of Motion after long hours of observing and testing the patterns of objects in motion. Newton's laws have become important to many aspects of life—from world travel to personal comforts in our homes.

Newton's laws provide the basis for many discoveries and technological advances we often take for granted. Airplanes fly because the lift created by their huge wings and powerful engines overcomes the force of gravity. Cars can travel well in

All around us, our world is constantly in motion.

Fast Fact

Most crime laboratories do not keep a physicist on staff full time. Rather than hire a physicist, some laboratories cross-train one of their criminalists—the people that examine crime scenes and trace evidence—to handle the analysis of blood spatter and other important physical evidence.

excess of 200 miles per hour because of advances in *aerodynamics* and engine design. The power produced by the gas engine can push the car down the road at high speed even though wind resistance increases with the increasing speed of the car.

The Laws of Motion form the basis for much of the field of natural science we know as physics. Technically speaking, physics is the science of motion. Any object that can move can be examined using the principles of physics. Keep in mind that there are objects that people cannot see. Photons—the tiny particles of light that travel from a light source to our eyes—move so fast that we cannot follow their movement.

Physics is a very useful science, since the motion of objects is of great concern to many people. The theories and formulas

Physics and the laws of motion predict how we would fall.

A forensic physicist can uncover how a burglar moved through a crime scene.

that are the backbone of physics have expanded over the years, as they have with other sciences. Technology has allowed researchers to look ever closer at the physical world, and the advances have been beneficial to everyone, not just the hardcore scientists of the world. One way that advances in physics have been good for the common person is through developments made in forensic science.

USING PHYSICS TO SOLVE CRIMES

Forensic experts must often use their knowledge of physics to help investigators understand what occurred at a crime scene. Physics can be used any time there is evidence that hinges on understanding how something moved before, during, or after the commission of a crime. Most often, the way an object or individual moved through a crime scene is used to reconstruct what happened. A knowledgeable forensic expert looks at the crime scene for a number of types of evidence that can provide valuable clues about the crime.

Cases where a weapon is swung, a bullet flies through the air, or a bomb explodes are all examples of the sort of attacks in which a knowledge of physics is useful for investigating the crime. Unfortunately, gun violence is found all around the world, and the instance of bomb blasts has increased as international terrorism has grown. A physicist is trained to examine the evidence to determine where a bomb was placed, or from what direction a bullet was fired. Energy of impact is a very important factor in some cases, and without physics, there would be no way to determine energy.

Energy can be a great indicator of the attacker's intent, as seen in the story of Carl Gustafson. The testimony of a physics expert can often be vital to the prosecution's case against a person trying to claim self-defense as Bell did. Something as simple as the direction that blood spatters can tell the entire story of a crime.

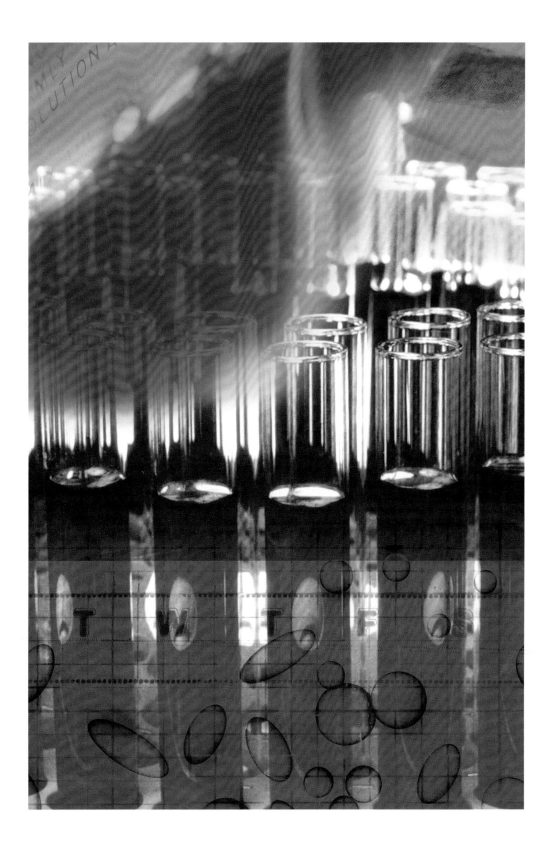

CHAPTER THREE

All About Blood

On July 16, 2004, Lori Hacking received a phone call at work. Witnesses couldn't tell what was discussed during that call, but Hacking was clearly upset and left work early.

Friends and family members, other than her husband, report last seeing her around 9:00 two days later. A clerk at a convenience store said he saw Lori and her husband that afternoon. Lori's husband, Mark, made a phone call to police on July 19 to report that she had not returned from an early-morning jog. He had gone out earlier that morning to buy a new mattress, and claimed his wife was not home when he came back. In the kitchen of their home, however, police discovered blood consistent with a stabbing. It appeared someone had tried to clean up the bloodstain using soap and water. Eventually, Mark Hacking was charged with aggravated murder. A short time later, Lori's body was found in a local landfill—but her blood had told its tale days earlier.

ALL ABOUT BLOOD: WHY IT DOES WHAT IT DOES

Many of the violent crimes committed each day involve the spilling of some amount of blood. It could be a few tiny drops, or the entire amount in a person's body. An experienced crime-scene investigator knows that different types of blood spatter tell different tales about the crime. But how do investigators and forensic experts know the differences? It begins with a thorough understanding of blood and human anatomy.

CHARACTERISTICS OF BLOOD

The popular saying goes: blood is thicker than water. This is very true. Many different types of molecules, each with a spe-

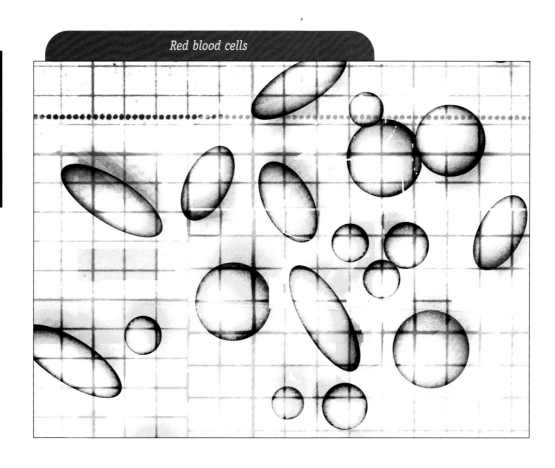

Red blood cells

Fast Facts About Blood

- The average human body contains approximately six quarts (5.7 liters) of blood.

- In one day, blood travels nearly 12,000 miles (19,312 kilometers).

- A human heart beats about 35 million times a year, pushing blood through the body's vessels.

cific job, make up blood, so blood is a very thick liquid because of this mixture of components. The various cells themselves are not liquid; they are actually solids suspended in a liquid called plasma—the clear fluid that gives blood its a liquid character. In humans, about 55 percent of the volume of blood is plasma. The red blood cells are the part of blood that gives it a reddish color. Blood also contains white blood cells and *platelets*, which are necessary for a person to be healthy.

Blood behaves in a unique fashion when it drips, gushes, or squirts on different surfaces. When blood is discovered at a crime scene, an analysis of the spatter patterns can reveal a surprising amount of information about the crime. The chemical properties of blood are an important part of the reason why it spatters as it does, but they also provide critical information for determining whether a sample really is a useful specimen of human blood. Taking the time to check the chemical properties is a very important step in blood analysis.

After screening the blood sample to determine that it is important to the case, the real examination of the blood can begin. Often, the samples are sent to two or three different departments of the central crime laboratory. Blood is a good source of DNA, a powerful piece of evidence when establishing identity. Most blood is also tested to determine the blood type of the subject who lost it. The forensic physicist is not concerned with the DNA or blood type, though. She wants to see the way the blood was found because the patterns of droplets

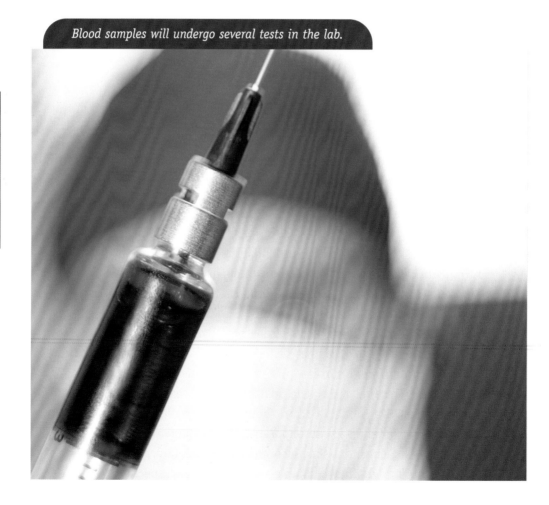

Blood samples will undergo several tests in the lab.

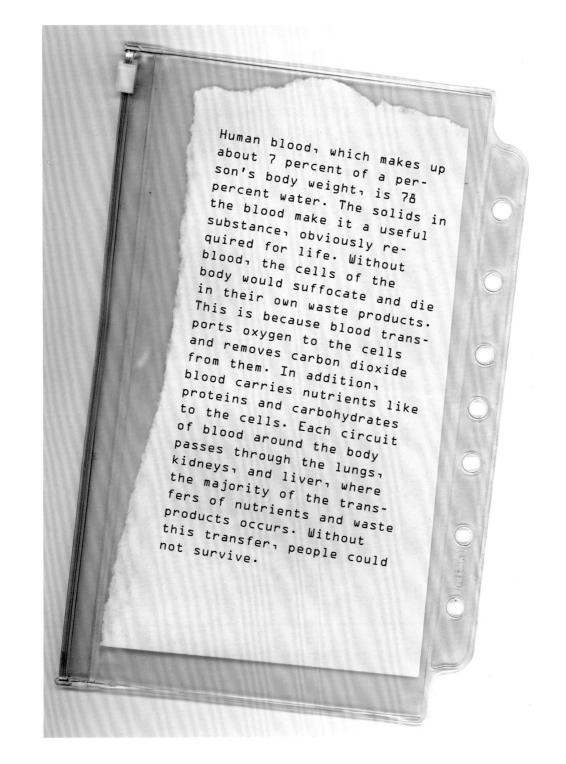

Human blood, which makes up about 7 percent of a person's body weight, is 78 percent water. The solids in the blood make it a useful substance, obviously required for life. Without blood, the cells of the body would suffocate and die in their own waste products. This is because blood transports oxygen to the cells and removes carbon dioxide from them. In addition, blood carries nutrients like proteins and carbohydrates to the cells. Each circuit of blood around the body passes through the lungs, kidneys, and liver, where the majority of the transfers of nutrients and waste products occurs. Without this transfer, people could not survive.

or spray can tell her a detailed story about what happened there.

Because blood is so thick, it does not flow as quickly down a surface as other fluids might. In addition, it tends to react in specific ways when striking different surfaces. One nice thing is that most people have blood of exactly the same composition. A key aspect of blood chemistry is that human blood always has about the same *viscosity*—it is nearly always about the same consistency. Blood, being a relatively viscous fluid, does not flow quickly when compared to water, which is a non-viscous liquid.

The chemical composition of blood gives it a large amount of surface tension—the molecules that make up blood are attracted to one another, so they tend to stick to each other. This

Blood is a viscous fluid that flows slower than water.

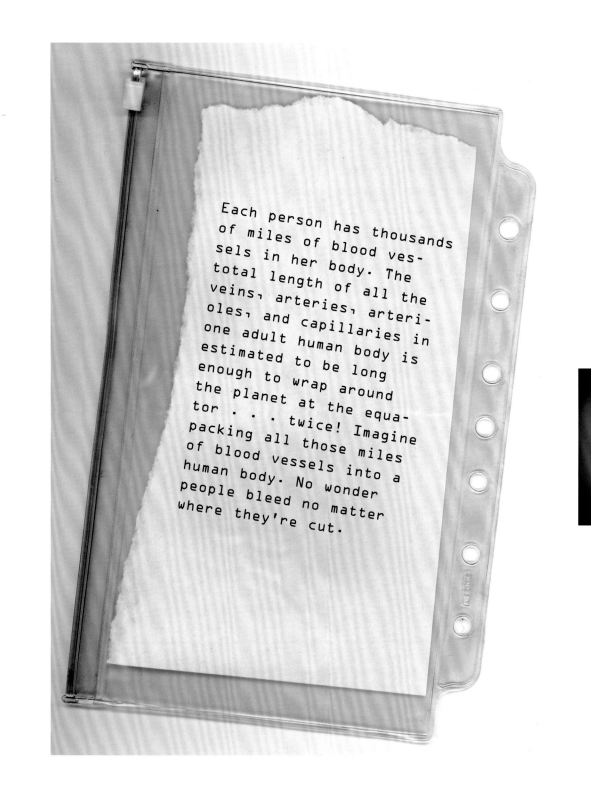

Each person has thousands of miles of blood vessels in her body. The total length of all the veins, arteries, arterioles, and capillaries in one adult human body is estimated to be long enough to wrap around the planet at the equator . . . twice! Imagine packing all those miles of blood vessels into a human body. No wonder people bleed no matter where they're cut.

is why blood behaves as it does when it runs down a surface; the high surface tension keeps the blood in droplets even as it moves down a surface. Liquids with low surface tension tend to break up as they fall down a surface.

THE BIOLOGY OF BLOOD FLOW

Blood is kept within the circulatory system under extreme pressure. A cut to a major blood vessel can result in a gush of blood spraying more than ten feet (3 meters) from the body.

The main organ of blood circulation is the heart, a very powerful and precise muscle that pumps constantly to keep our blood flowing. Blood flowing away from the heart is usually rich in oxygen and under the greatest pressure. Arteries are muscular blood vessels that carry blood away from the heart to the tissues of the body. After the blood has released its load of oxygen, it flows back toward the heart through the veins. Thinner walled than arteries, veins are not usually under quite the same amount of pressure. This is not to say that a wound to a major vein will not bleed heavily; it certainly will. A deep gash to a major vein, such as the *superior vena cava*, will result in a person losing enough blood to bleed to death in only a few minutes.

The largest and most muscular blood vessel in a person's body is the aorta. This huge artery runs down through the ribcage and toward our legs, where it splits into smaller arteries that supply blood to the legs. A wound that opens the aorta will often result in death within seconds, not minutes.

Blood spatter analysis requires a sound understanding of human anatomy. This is because the amount of energy behind a spray or gush of blood can be directly related to the circumstances of the wound—where the wound is on the body, the type of weapon used to inflict the wound, and the exact damage done to the body by the wound.

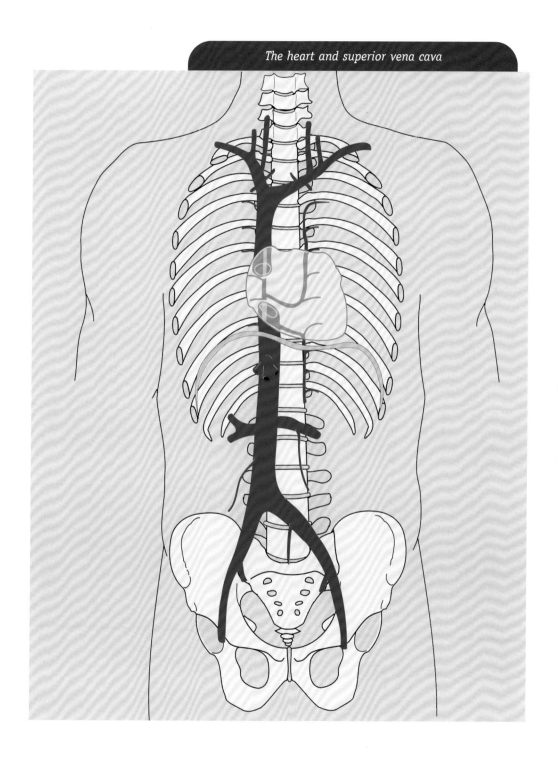

47

48

Blood pressure is a factor in the amount of blood a person loses when they are cut deeply. Blood pressure is controlled by two main factors: the individual's heart and the muscles of the major blood vessels.

Arteries, being muscular tubes, can contract and reduce the amount of space within themselves in response to instructions from the brain. Under stressful conditions, the blood vessels contract to force an increase in the rate of blood flow, which in turn increases the rate of oxygen transfer to the cells. When a person is frightened, the need for additional oxygen to the cells is obvious. More oxygen means the person is better able to flee or fight.

THE WAYS WE LOSE BLOOD: PASSIVE VS. PROJECTED BLOOD

Not all wounds are created equal: some cuts bleed more than others. A number of different types of blood loss are commonly associated with crime scenes, each with characteristics that differentiate them from the others. The type of blood loss is important information to investigators because it can be used to make an educated guess about whether the wound was inflicted intentionally, inflicted by accident, or self-inflicted.

In general, there are two main types of blood loss. Oozing blood is the slowest and is most commonly found with shallow surface wounds like scrapes. Generally speaking, oozing blood

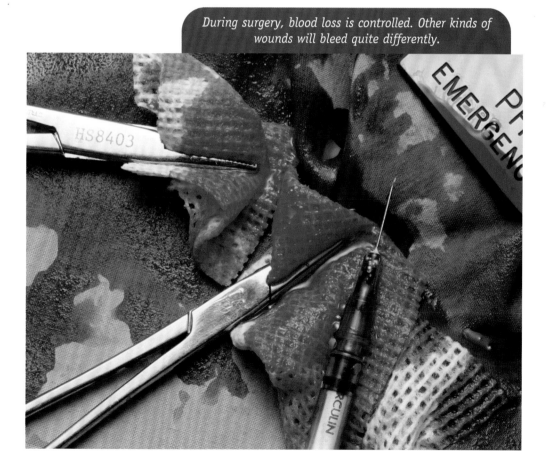

During surgery, blood loss is controlled. Other kinds of wounds will bleed quite differently.

Image 1

does not cause spatter unless it flows for a long time. In these cases, it can drip off the person's body and fall to the floor, leaving behind a telltale trail of drops. Oozing blood often has some small clots in it because blood tends to begin clotting as soon as a person is cut.

Forensic experts usually call blood that falls straight to the ground from a victim passive blood loss. Drips and oozing are passive because there is no energy from the body moving them out away from the source. Passive blood sometimes drips off in one location, each drop falling on top of the last, or in a trail as the wounded person moves.

When a major blood vessel is damaged, blood often sprays out strongly. Blood that sprays out in large amounts is called gushing or spurting blood. Gushing blood is the main source of what forensic scientists call projected blood, which means that energy forced the blood out of a person's body. Projected blood can spray for a long distance because of blood pressure. In addition, because of the high pressure, a gush of blood can contain an impressive amount of fluid. People who are gushing blood obviously need medical attention, but because of the severity of the injury, it is not uncommon for someone in that condition to remain at the crime scene. Unfortunately, it is also not uncommon for them to have died from blood loss by the time the police arrive. Image 1 is typical of an arterial gush from a major artery. The amount of blood lost was obviously huge.

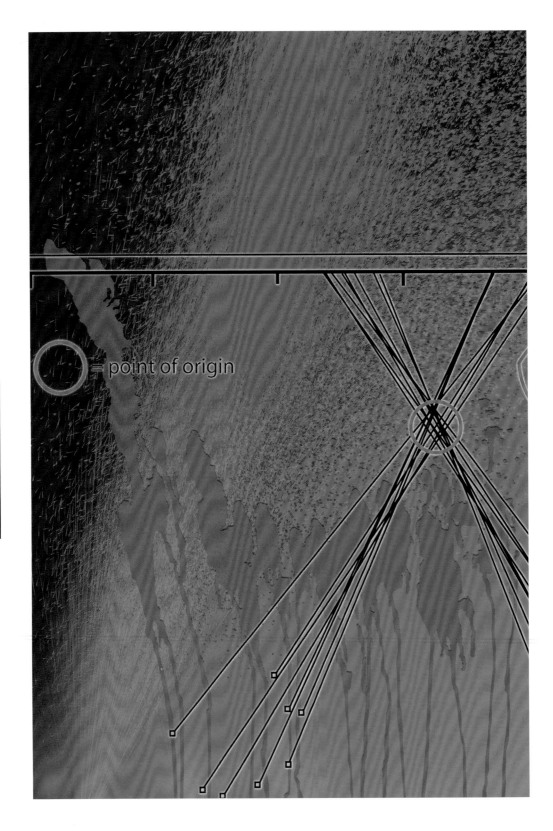

= point of origin

CHAPTER FOUR

Blood Spatter

O n September 2, 2003, someone entered the home of Alan and Diane Johnson and shot them both to death. Both victims had been shot at very close range, one bullet each. Their daughter, eighteen-year-old Sarah, had been sleeping elsewhere in the house and came running when she heard the gunshots. She called 911 immediately. Or so she would have the police believe.

Sarah, the prime suspect in the killings because of inconsistencies in her report to the police, insisted she was innocent in spite of the prosecution's belief. She had bruises on her shoulder that could have come from a brief struggle with her father, who had been shot in the chest while exiting the shower. Signs of a struggle were evident in the bathroom, indicating he had not died immediately from the wound. The bruise on her shoulder showed vertical marks that appeared to match the lines of the door casing on the inside of the bathroom.

Diane was in bed when she was shot once in the head. Investigators had some difficulty determining whether she had

the comforter pulled over her head when she was shot, a factor that would have affected the way the blood flew when the shot was fired.

The defense team hung their case on the hope that they could shed doubt on Sarah's guilt because of the lack of blood spatter on her clothing that morning. The defense attorneys believed there was no way a person could shoot someone at close range without being covered by the victim's blood.

Prosecutors felt they had more than enough evidence to convict Sarah Johnson on two counts of first-degree murder. First of all, the killings were premeditated because the

Sufficient evidence leads to convictions.

Johnsons had been killed when they were most vulnerable. Second, forensic experts had found Alan's and Diane's blood and DNA on the bathrobe Sarah admitted wearing that morning. Third, she had a motive: her mother had recently forbid her to date a nineteen-year-old school dropout, leading to a heated argument between mother and daughter. Finally, Sarah had been in the guesthouse on the premises the day before, and a Winchester rifle had been taken that day. That same gun had been used in the killing.

The defense strategy failed; Sarah was convicted of both counts of murder. The defense expert who was called to testify on her behalf with regard to the blood-spatter evidence was unable to convince the jury that there was no way she could have fired the gun from that range and not been covered in tiny spatters.

EXAMINING BLOOD SPATTER: PUTTING TOGETHER A PUZZLE

A number of blood-spatter patterns can usually be found at the scene of a crime. These patterns are the source of much of the information used to reconstruct the events. Blood-spatter patterns are very much like a puzzle—by putting together all of the pieces in the correct places, an investigator can usually determine a great deal about the crime. A detailed examination of individual spatter patterns, including their positions and orientations at the scene, can provide investigators with information such as:

- the position of the victim at the time of the attack

- whether the blood flowed out in spurts or gushed slowly

- how hard the blow that caused the bleeding was

- how many blows fell

- sometimes, where the attacker was standing during the attack

A number of important factors can have a significant effect on a spatter pattern. Using principles of physics, an investigator can determine the angle of impact of the blood droplets. Droplets that fall straight down onto a surface typically leave nearly circular stains where they fall. As the angle changes from 90°, the spatter stains become more elongated. Calculations of the ratio of the width to the length of the droplet can determine the approximate angle at which the droplet hit the surface. Longer droplets indicate lower angles of impact.

When a moving blood droplet hits a surface it usually splashes forward (Image 2). The strong surface tension of the

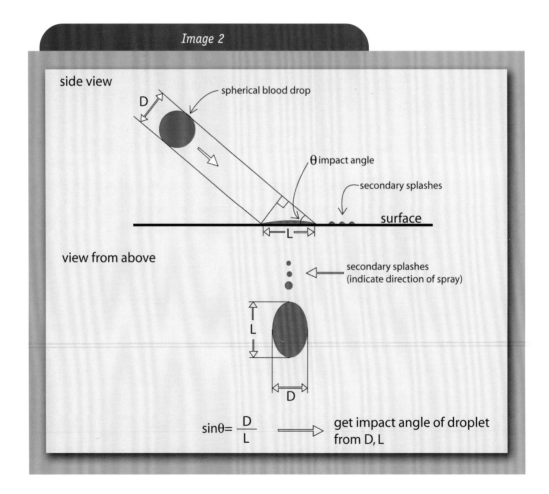

Image 2

side view

D

spherical blood drop

θ impact angle

secondary splashes

surface

L

view from above

secondary splashes
(indicate direction of spray)

L

D

$\sin\theta = \dfrac{D}{L}$ ⟹ get impact angle of droplet from D, L

blood holds most of the droplet together, but the energy of the impact can break off small amounts of blood that splash farther forward. Normally there will be one large parent droplet and one or more *satellite* droplets left on the surface. A quick examination of the location of the parent droplet and the satellite droplets can tell an investigator from which direction the droplet came. The satellite droplets always continue along the same line as the direction of travel of the blood. In other words, the satellite droplets will be found farther along the line of travel than the parent droplet. If a line were drawn through the satellite spatters back through the center of the parent droplet, it would point in the direction from where the blood originated. Image 3 is a depiction of what a blood droplet moving as it hit a surface would look like. The elongated spine at

Image 3

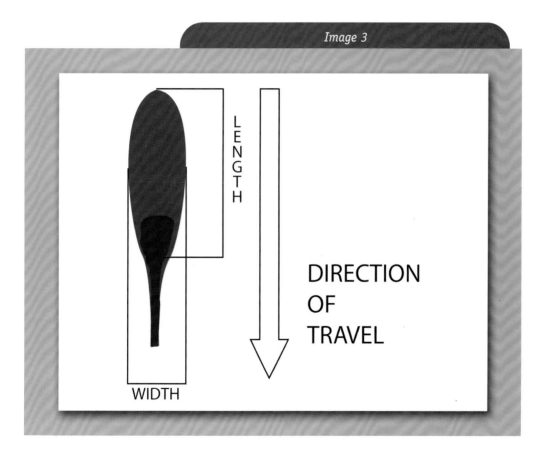

LENGTH

DIRECTION
OF
TRAVEL

WIDTH

A proper analysis of blood-spatter patterns can yield a surprising amount of information about the crime. Among the easily identified facts that can be determined by examining blood-spatter patterns are the positions of the victim, assailant, and objects at the scene. In addition, the type of weapon used to cause the spatter can sometimes be determined by looking at the wound and the sorts of spatter present. Multiple spatters can indicate the number of blows, shots, stabs, or other attacks that occurred. The movement and direction of victim and assailant after bloodshed began is usually readily apparent. Among the most crucial evidence is the ability to determine what events occurred and in what sequence they occurred. This can be vital to a prosecution.

the end of the droplet indicates the direction the droplet was moving when it impacted the surface.

In addition to direction of travel, an investigator can usually determine the amount of energy behind the droplets by looking at their overall size. Generally, small droplets are the result of higher energy projecting them outward from their source. This information is particularly important in the case of violent attacks; determining the amount of energy can indicate how hard a victim was hit. It is usually very difficult for a suspect to argue he did not intend to injure someone if it can be shown that the blow to the victim was extremely hard.

Blood droplets from a single source do not necessarily all end up in one area of the crime scene. If the victim was moving when hit, or if the assailant moved around the victim, the blood is found in a *radius* around the location or path of the

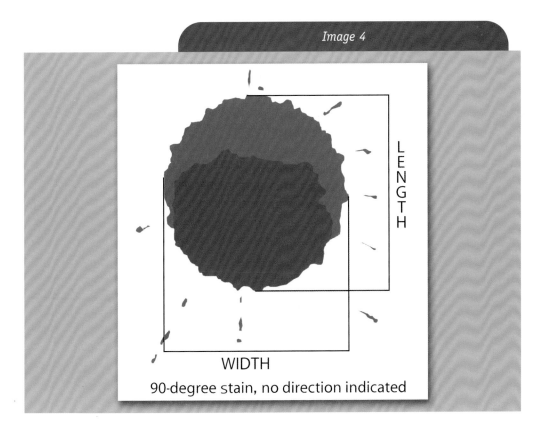

Image 4

LENGTH

WIDTH

90-degree stain, no direction indicated

victim. Close examination of the pattern can be used to reconstruct where the victim was for each blow. Sometimes, a model is built of the crime scene to aid in the reconstruction of the crime. The forensic expert places drawings or pictures of each blood droplet in the model and then uses string to retrace the path of flight of the droplets from the source. Image 4 is a sample crime-scene reconstruction common to the process used to trace the path of blood droplets.

A forensic physicist can easily determine the point of origin of blood droplets by drawing lines through each individual droplet back along the path from which it came. The place where the lines converge, or come together, is the point of origin. Each point of origin at a crime scene is indicative of a

Image 5

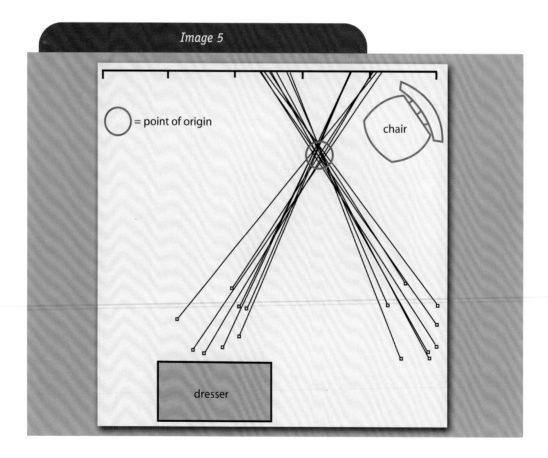

◯ = point of origin

chair

dresser

source of blood spatter. At this point, it does not matter to the forensic scientist whether the blood came from the victim or the criminal; she is just trying to determine the location of the origin of the blood. Image 5 is an illustration of a typical analysis done to determine the point of origin of blood spatter. Take note of the multiple convergence points. This indicates blood was spilled from two different locations at this particular crime scene.

SURFACE MATTERS: HARD VS. SOFT SURFACES

Blood does not act the same way when it falls on all surfaces; what matters is how porous the surface is. There is a spectrum

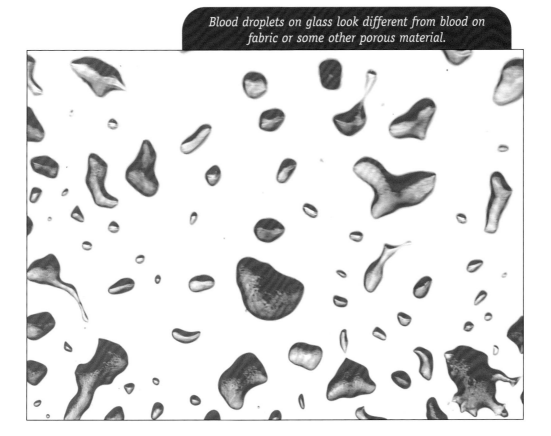

Blood droplets on glass look different from blood on fabric or some other porous material.

of surface types that are commonly found at crime scenes, each with a different effect on droplet formation. It is the job of a forensic expert to know the differences. If the surface is very smooth and nonporous, like glass, blood usually stays in a relatively tight drop on the surface. The surface tension of the blood keeps it together. If the surface is porous, like brick, the blood droplet tends to break up more on impact. In this case, the outer edges of the droplet will look more ragged and variable. Blood droplets with smooth edges are the result of impact with a smooth, nonporous surface.

A floor covering such as linoleum usually results in a slight splashing outward of the blood. Linoleum is slightly porous, so it causes more edge distortion than glass but less than concrete or brick. Image 6 is a spatter that resulted from blood

Image 6

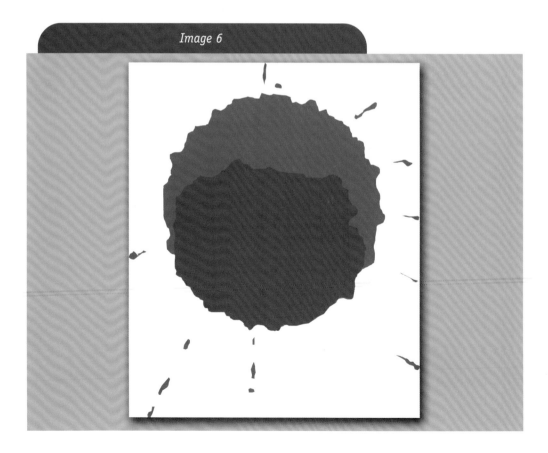

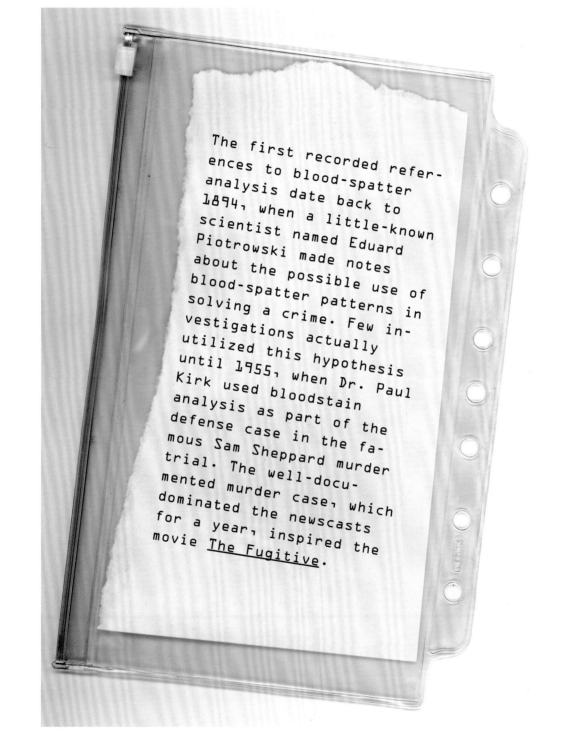

The first recorded references to blood-spatter analysis date back to 1894, when a little-known scientist named Eduard Piotrowski made notes about the possible use of blood-spatter patterns in solving a crime. Few investigations actually utilized this hypothesis until 1955, when Dr. Paul Kirk used bloodstain analysis as part of the defense case in the famous Sam Sheppard murder trial. The well-documented murder case, which dominated the newscasts for a year, inspired the movie <u>The Fugitive</u>.

63

dropping from about five feet (1.5 meters) directly down onto a linoleum floor. Look at the edges of the droplet. They have been slightly distorted by the impact with the nonporous floor.

It can be difficult to determine which direction a spatter came from when blood falls on some surfaces. For example, droplets tend to splash less predictably when they fall on surfaces with inconsistencies, such as rough cut wood. An analysis is still possible, just more time consuming. Sometimes an

Image 7

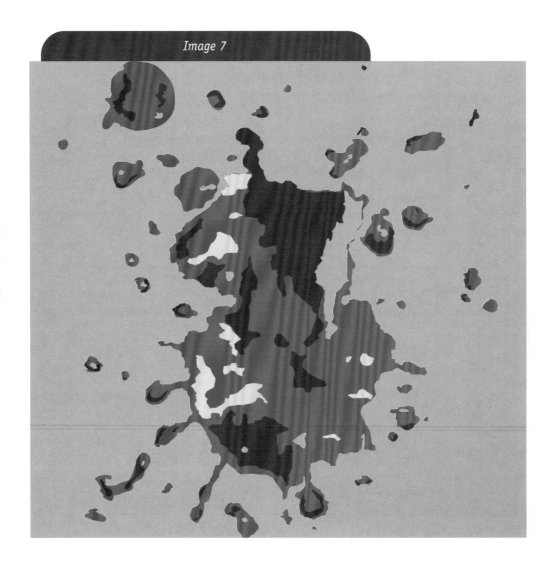

expert will take a sample of the surface and do several test reenactments of spilling blood. Information gathered in this way can usually help the scientist decipher the patterns. Image 7 is a typical spatter mark on a nonporous surface. Notice the irregularity of the edges and satellite spatters.

ENERGY MATTERS: HIGH-, MEDIUM-, AND LOW-ENERGY SPATTERS

The amount of energy used to spatter blood makes a big difference in the appearance of individual spatter marks. In the interest of gathering as much information as possible, determining the approximate amount of energy falls under the tasks of the forensic physicist. Courts usually allow testimony relating to the amount of energy behind an attack as evidence of the intent of the attacker. Accidental attacks are not often very hard impacts.

There are three categories of impact energy: high, medium, and low. Each has a different effect on the size and shape of blood droplets. In general, as the energy of the impact increases, the size of individual droplets decreases. An object moving at more than 100 feet (30.4 meters) per second when it hits the victim causes high-energy spatter. Blood droplets created by high-energy spatter are usually one millimeter in diameter or smaller. This sort of spatter is commonly associated with gunshot wounds and bomb blasts because of the high speed needed to create them. Most other objects just do not move that fast. Image 8 is a picture of the blood-spatter stain left when a bullet passed through a victim. The individual droplets are very small. An inspection of the shape of the droplets indicates the spatter flew directly onto the surface in the picture.

An object traveling between five- and twenty-five feet (between 1.5 and 7.6 meters) per second when it hits an individual causes medium-impact spatters. Individual spatter marks in a medium-velocity spatter stain are usually between one and four millimeters in diameter. Most violent attacks with blunt objects result in medium-impact spatter stains. Swipe patterns, as shown in Image 9, can also reveal information about the crime.

Large quantities of blood are a common aspect of low-impact spatters. Low-impact spatters are relatively common at crime scenes, since they can be created by large quantities of blood falling onto the ground or floor. In general, as long as the force behind the spatter is moving at less than five feet (1.5 meters) per second, it results in low-impact spatter. These stains are commonly greater than four millimeters in diameter because the energy behind the impact is not high enough to

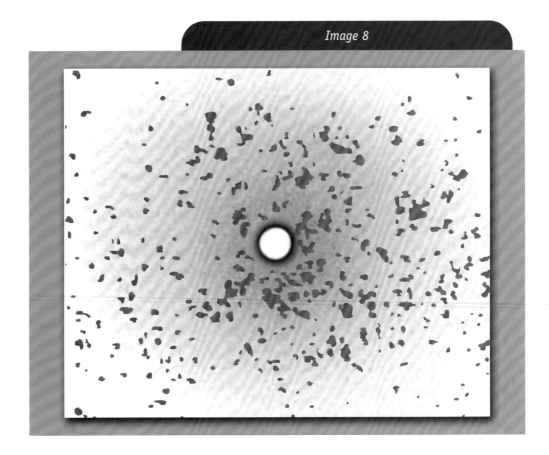

Image 8

break the surface tension of the blood. Image 10 shows low-impact spatter. Notice the many satellite spatters around the parent spatter.

SPATTER FROM A MOVING OBJECT: CAST-OFF SPATTER

When an attacker uses a handheld weapon and takes more than one swing, blood often clings to the weapon and is scattered by the back-and-forth motion of the weapon. Imagine swinging a baseball bat. A good swing pulls the bat through an arc to the target. In order to swing again, the bat must be pulled back and readied again. The same is true if the bat were used as a weapon. Each swing passes along an arc between the attacker and the victim. The motion of the swing causes blood clinging to the bat to fly off.

68

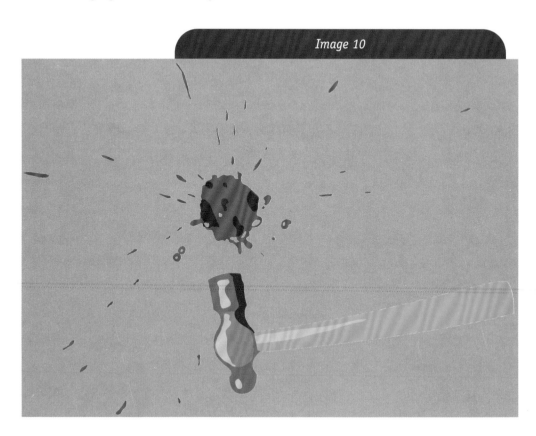

Image 10

In crime fighting, few developments have had as large an impact as the personal computer. Most aspects of forensic science have been affected in one way or another by advancements in computer technology. Blood-spatter analysis is no exception. In recent years software has been developed that allows a forensic expert to use digital photographs of the crime scene to assist in analysis. Finding a single point of origin is often made much easier by the use of computer imagery. In fact, some programs even perform calculations on their own to draw trajectory lines without any user input.

Blood that is left behind by more than one swing is called cast-off or back spatter. It is common for a forensic investigator to find cast-off spatter on the walls or even the ceiling of a crime scene where a weapon was used. Cast-off spatter is indicative of multiple blows, so it is very important information in court. Accidental injuries do not normally leave behind back spatter because accidents usually involve only one swing. Hitting a person more than once with a weapon is a dead giveaway of intent to cause harm. Image 11 is a depiction of a typical cast-off spatter pattern. To determine point of origin, the cast off from the end of the weapon can be traced in the same way as most other spatter patterns, allowing the investigator to figure out where the attacker was standing during the attack. In addition, the approximate height from the ground of the weapon can be determined through examination of cast-off patterns.

Secondary spatters are known as cast-off or back spatter.

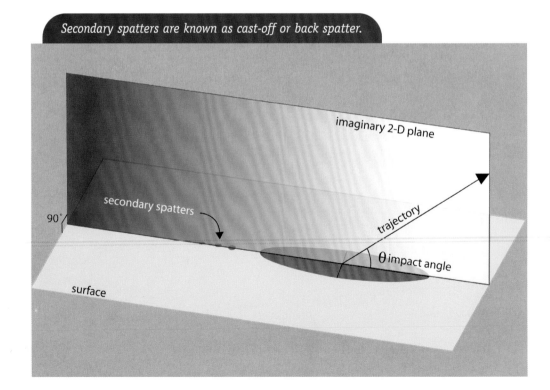

AMOUNT OF BLOOD
ALSO MATTERS

Examinations of blood spatter must take into account the amount of blood lost by the victim. As more and more blood falls in one location, the amount of spatter from that point increases because of the splashing that occurs when one drop falls onto another. Pooling blood from a slowly dripping wound usually has many satellite spatters surrounding it. The energy of the drops is dependent on the height of their fall—the higher the source, the more energy the drops will have when they hit the ground. Satellite spatter that is far from the parent droplet indicates the source was high off the ground. Understanding the effect of an increasing amount of blood on the spatter pattern helps during investigations of these sorts of spatters. Image 12 shows a sample pattern created when multiple drops of blood fell on one single spot. The number of

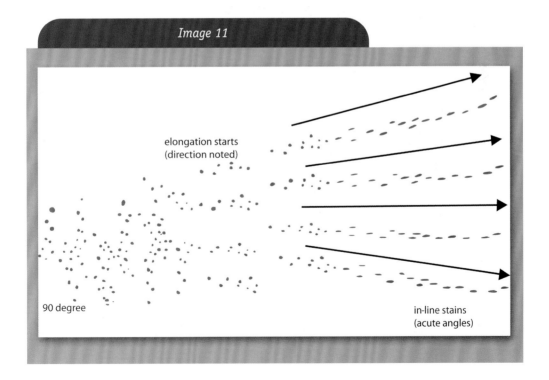

Image 11

elongation starts
(direction noted)

90 degree

in-line stains
(acute angles)

Image 12

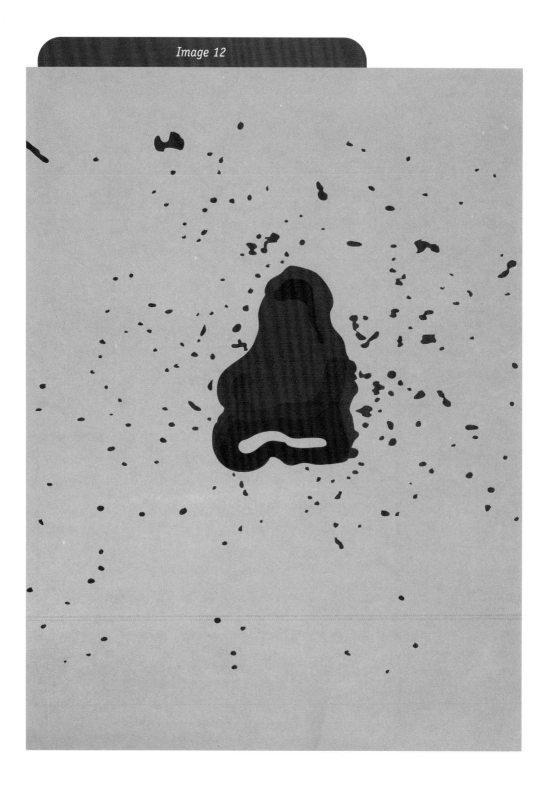

satellite spatters increases as more and more drops fall on the parent droplet.

Much information goes into being a specialist in the interpretation of blood spatters. In fact, blood-spatter evidence alone could be enough to keep a laboratory full of scientists busy every day of the year. It becomes more and more apparent that splitting a forensic laboratory into many departments is the best way to deal with the different evidence types gathered on a daily basis.

CHAPTER FIVE

Using Physics: Rifling and Ballistics

On April 15, 1920, in South Braintree, Massachusetts, two men shot and killed a paymaster and his guard in a robbery. They grabbed more than $16,000 and fled in a dark touring car with several other men.

The ground inside the bank was littered with spent shell casings. The getaway car was soon found, abandoned nearby. Police believed the man behind the killings and robbery was Mike Boda, but by the time they found where he lived, he had fled for Italy.

The police arrested two of Boda's friends, Nicola Sacco and Bartolomeo Vanzetti, men who matched physical descriptions of the killers. When arrested, Sacco was carrying a .32 Colt automatic, and Vanzetti had a .38 Harrington & Richardson in his possession. The gun Sacco carried matched the caliber of the weapon used in the killings. Vanzetti's gun matched the gun the paymaster was believed to have on him when he was murdered. Sacco and Vanzetti were put on trial and found guilty for the murders of the paymaster and his guard.

The murder trial of the two men hinged on evidence gathered from the bullets found in the bodies of the paymaster and

security guard. The prosecution and defense each hired "expert" witnesses to speak about the value of the bullets as evidence, but neither had any scientific experience. Their testimony was largely based on guesses they made.

The jury looked over the evidence for hours, comparing the characteristics on "Bullet III" and on the barrel of the Colt taken from Sacco. In the end, the jury determined that the bullet had to have come from Sacco's gun.

WHEN GUNS ARE USED FOR CRIME

When a crime involves the use of a firearm, it is important for the forensic scientist examining the evidence to gather as much information as possible about the gun used in the commission of the crime. Similar to the Principle of Exchange, most

Guns often have unique individual traits.

guns *impart* a sort of fingerprint on every bullet that passes through their barrel and on the spent shell casings of the fired cartridges. The term used for these identifying marks is *rifling*. This is the sort of evidence that contributed to the Sacco and Vanzetti case.

It is often possible to use physical examinations of the gun, bullets, and casings found at the crime scene to determine whether a specific gun was used in the crime. Linking a gun to a crime scene is a good way to start the process of connecting a particular person to the shooting. If ownership, and more important, possession, can be established, the gun can become very strong evidence against a suspect.

The identifying characteristics of a gun are dependent on the lands—raised edges—and grooves the manufacturer builds into the inside of the barrel to help improve the gun's accuracy. A bullet that spirals as it comes out of the barrel is much more accurate than one that does not. Gun manufacturers use unique patterns of lands and grooves based on their research, so it is not uncommon for guns from two different makers to have different ballistic patterns right out of the box.

MORE THAN JUST A GUN FINGERPRINT

Understanding the physics of gunfire and bullet paths is valuable knowledge for a forensic firearms examiner. Most shooters use physics when they fire their guns, even if they don't understand the science behind it. The study of movements and forces involved in the propulsion of objects through the air is known as *ballistics*. Everyone knows that bullets will fall to the ground eventually as they travel away from the gun—a phenomenon known as bullet drop. The rapid burning of the gunpowder in the cartridge provides the energy necessary to fire the bullet. The farther from the gun the bullet goes, the slower it travels—it slows from friction with the air. These factors are useful for a forensic expert trying to determine from where a bullet was fired. The direction of bullet travel is usually not

Most major bullet manufacturers willingly provide the FBI with data about their bullets and the expected flight paths of a bullet fired from a gun. In addition, the powders used to load the cartridges are recorded so that if the bullet is used in a crime, a chemical analysis can determine the composition of the gunpowder, leading the forensic experts back to the company that manufactured the bullet. This sort of evidence can link an individual to a crime if investigators can prove he had bullets of the same make in his possession.

hard for a forensic expert to establish. In much the same way a point of origin can be determined for blood spatter, a bullet path can often be established by examining the points of entry and exit and drawing a straight line back along the suspected path of travel.

Bullet energy is the amount of energy transferred from the bullet to the victim on impact. It is a useful figure because a ballistics expert can sometimes use it to determine how far the bullet traveled before it hit the target. The amount of bullet energy decreases with increasing distance from the gun, and

Energy transfers from bullet to object on impact.

depending on the shape and size of the bullet itself, a ballistics expert can calculate how far it flew. Because bullets drop as they move forward, being able to calculate the distance from the shooter to the target can sometimes provide useful information for determining the assailant's location.

When investigators find a bullet at a crime scene, either in a victim or lodged in some other object, the ballistics expert can usually identify the manufacturer relatively easily. Most major bullet manufacturers imprint their bullets with a mark that is unique to their company, so identification is a simple matter of finding the mark and matching it to sample bullets from each company. This sounds tedious—and it used to be in the days before the use of computer-database information storage. Today, a computerized search can find a match very quickly, saving the analyst valuable time.

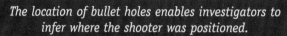

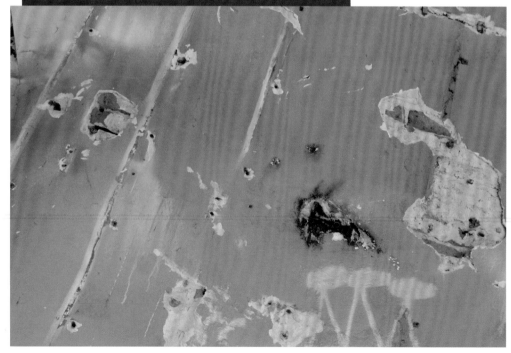

The location of bullet holes enables investigators to infer where the shooter was positioned.

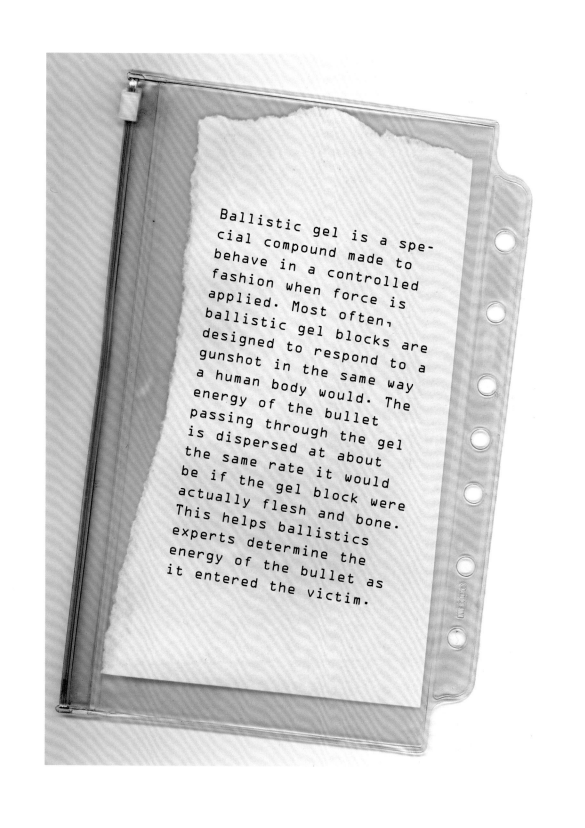

Ballistic gel is a spe-
cial compound made to
behave in a controlled
fashion when force is
applied. Most often,
ballistic gel blocks are
designed to respond to a
gunshot in the same way
a human body would. The
energy of the bullet
passing through the gel
is dispersed at about
the same rate it would
be if the gel block were
actually flesh and bone.
This helps ballistics
experts determine the
energy of the bullet as
it entered the victim.

82

Matching the bullet to a specific gun helps investigators find the assailant.

A similar method can be used to identify the make of the gun used. The FBI maintains a database of manufacturer-provided information about the markings guns leave on bullets and shell casings. Identification of the gun is vital, because a bullet fired from one gun may not have the same flight characteristics as the same bullet fired from a different gun. The energy the bullet has as it leaves the barrel depends on such things as the length of the barrel and the shape of the firing chamber in the gun.

After identifying the companies that produced the bullet and the gun, a ballistics expert can begin testing to determine the energy of the bullet as it leaves the barrel of the gun. For this, a special ballistic gel is used. Using the same brand of gun as is suspected (or in some cases known) to have been used in the crime, the expert points the gun at the gel and fires a bullet into it from a set distance, usually about ten feet (3 meters). The bullet blasts into the gel, *expending* energy as it goes. The distance it travels in the gel is then used to calculate the energy the bullet had as it left the gun. With this information, estimates can be made of the distance the bullet found at the crime scene traveled from its point of origin.

The laws that govern how things move and how energy is expended give crime investigators many clues. The laws of physics apply not only to how bullets behave but also to bombs and other explosions.

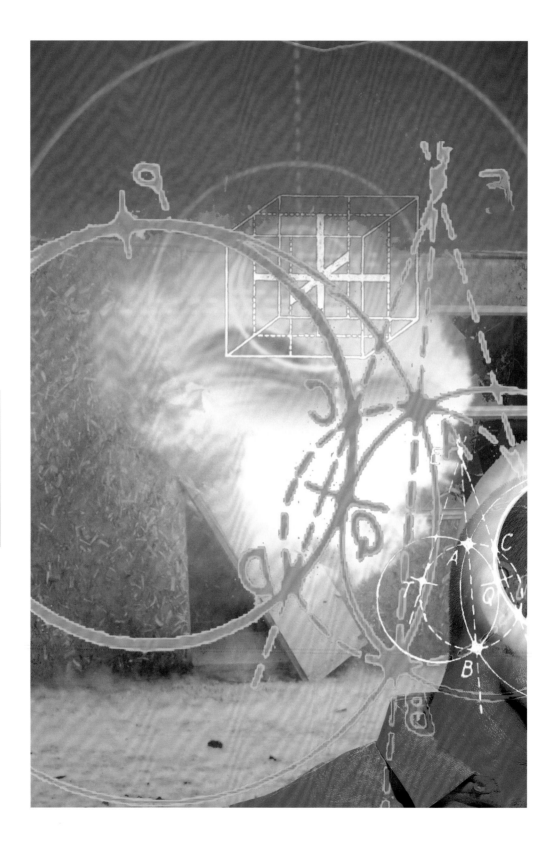

CHAPTER SIX

Using Physics: Bombs and Explosions

One of the most infamous days in American history surrounds the largest bomb blast ever detonated on American soil. American citizens Timothy McVeigh and Terry Nichols placed the bomb in Oklahoma City's Alfred P. Murrah Federal Building. The 5,000-pound bomb was designed to do one thing: kill people. The explosion blew away the north side of the building and resulted in 168 deaths. This building was chosen for a reason—it was the location of many government agencies, the target of these homegrown terrorists.

On April 19, 1995, Timothy McVeigh drove a rented moving truck to the front of the building and parked it, knowing the effect it would soon have on the lives of the people inside, and around the country. At 9:02 A.M., late enough in the day that the building would be filling with people, the bomb exploded, tearing apart the building and shaking the entire city. The blast damaged more than three hundred buildings in the surrounding area.

Once the smoke had cleared, a massive rescue effort was initiated. At the same time, the work of examining the evidence began. Bomb experts from around the country came to

work on the scene, hoping to help convict the men who had orchestrated the deadliest attack in the United States before September 11, 2001.

It soon became clear to experts that the bomb had been made from readily available commercial components, including racing fuel and ammonium nitrate, a fertilizer used on farms all around the country. An analysis of the energy generated by the explosion revealed the builders were very well versed in the dark art of bomb making.

BOMB EXPLOSIONS— DEADLY WEAPONS

Crimes are never nice, but using a bomb to commit one is particularly dastardly. A bomb is a very indiscriminate way to kill because, unlike a gun, a bomb is very difficult to aim at just one target. There are people who understand the way bombs work and how they can be carefully positioned to cause very little damage to anything but the intended target, but these people usually work in law enforcement or the military. Bombs are an interesting and deadly mix of physics and chemistry, and the people who understand how they work are usually very intelligent individuals with a sound understanding of both sciences.

Unfortunately, bombs are often detonated by individuals who know very little about physics; they may have the basic knowledge required to create the bomb, but they fail to comprehend how the bomb will behave once it explodes. The results may take them by surprise; in some cases, the explosion may even take the perpetrators' lives as well as their victims'.

The use of bombs has long been a favorite tactic of terrorists, both domestic and international. The damage a bomb can do is unmatched, both physically and mentally. Bombs have a very strong psychological effect on people, stirring up more fear than any other weapon used in a crime. The Olympic Village bomber in Atlanta, the militants behind the Oklahoma City bombing, and the terrorists who detonated a bomb in the lower level of the World Trade Center all preyed on the fears of innocent people to send their messages.

Along with all the other weapons of war that have found their way into the hands of criminals around the world, bomb-making technology has advanced in recent years. In response to the growing threat of bomb violence, there have been developments in the science used to examine the damage done when bombs are detonated. A number of agencies around the world maintain professional bomb squads, and forensic bomb experts can be found in a few major forensic laboratories around the United States.

Bombs and other explosives are becoming more common outside of war zones.

THE SCIENCE BEHIND THE BLAST

Everyone knows bombs are very destructive, but few people understand how they actually accomplish the damage they do. Chemicals inside the bomb are combined in such a way as to be very unstable, releasing huge amounts of energy when the conditions for their reaction are met. Sometimes the only thing that is needed is a tiny spark, which can be provided by a small battery connected to a timer. Once the reaction begins, there is often no stopping it. As the chemicals react, the bomb explodes.

When a bomb explodes, rapid expansion of the air surrounding the device causes a *shock wave*. Air is composed of molecules such as oxygen and nitrogen in their gaseous state

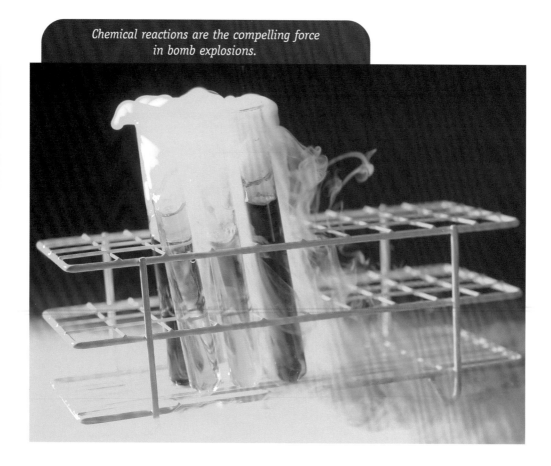

Chemical reactions are the compelling force in bomb explosions.

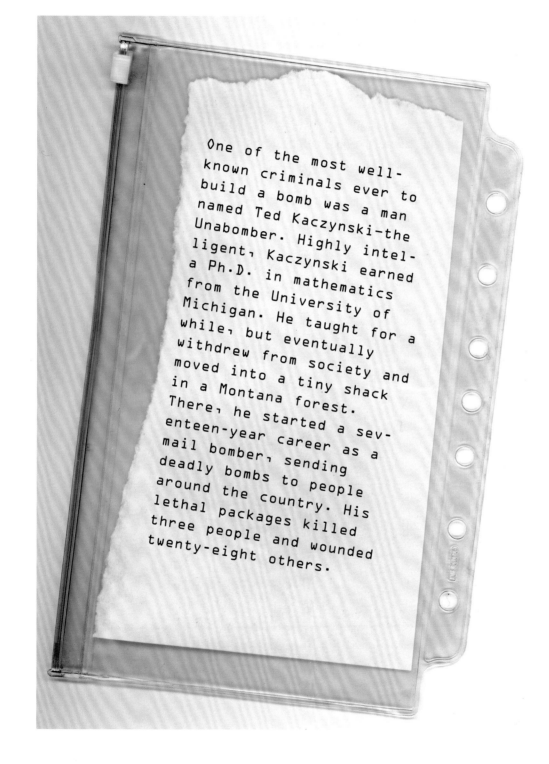

One of the most well-known criminals ever to build a bomb was a man named Ted Kaczynski—the Unabomber. Highly intelligent, Kaczynski earned a Ph.D. in mathematics from the University of Michigan. He taught for a while, but eventually withdrew from society and moved into a tiny shack in a Montana forest. There, he started a seventeen-year career as a mail bomber, sending deadly bombs to people around the country. His lethal packages killed three people and wounded twenty-eight others.

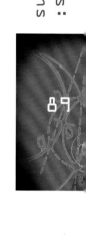

moving around in a random way. When chemicals in the bomb react with each other, the bomb releases a great deal of energy that moves away from the bomb very rapidly. This energy forces the air away from the bomb, causing the shock wave. Bigger bombs are not always more powerful, but the more powerful the bomb, the more violent the shock wave. The shock wave gradually loses energy as it moves out from the device, and structures nearby absorb some of the energy. Most bombs do damage in a short range, but the overall energy of the blast is the ultimate determinant of the distance the explosion can spread.

People who know how bombs work can examine a blast area and determine where the bomb that caused it was when it exploded and the approximate amount of energy released by the

A bomb site

The federal government maintains a department within the Department of Justice that is tasked with policing and preventing the public from violent crime. The Bureau of Alcohol, Tobacco, Firearms, and Explosives (ATF) is also charged with enforcing federal laws regarding alcohol, tobacco, firearms, explosives, and arson.

blast. In fact, it is possible to carefully design a bomb to release its energy in a chosen direction; it is a matter of knowing how the process works. A blast normally breaks through
the weakest part of the bomb's container. In pipe bombs, this
is often along the seam where the metal was rolled together
during production.

Bombers hoping to inflict the most destruction often add
objects like nails, ball bearings, or broken glass to their bombs
to increase damage done to people close to the explosion.
These bombs can be the worst kind because in addition to the
death and terror they cause, they sometimes leave maimed and
scarred people to cope with the damage.

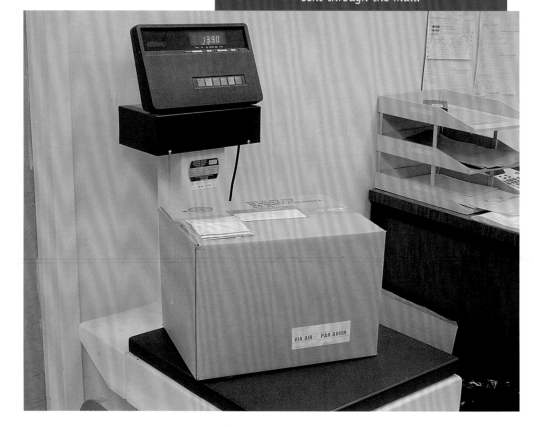

*Bombs may be inconspicuously packaged and
sent through the mail.*

EXAMINING BOMB BLASTS

Crime scenes where there have been explosions are very difficult to analyze. A massive amount of debris is often scattered around, and if people were present when the blast happened, the presence of bodies can add to the chaos. Consequently, an examination of a bomb site is not an easy task. Investigators usually start by figuring out where the bomb was placed. The expansion of the shock wave leaves behind a very telling pattern of damage that a person who understands the basics of physics can decipher. Like a blood-spatter pattern, the shock wave radiates outward from the point of origin, damaging whatever is in its path. It is sometimes more difficult to determine the direction of the shock wave's travel because of the cluttered aspect of most bomb sites. But once the direction is determined, it is easy enough to draw lines back along the direction of travel and find the place where they converge.

After finding the explosion's point of origin, the investigator can begin looking for pieces of the bomb itself. Normally, these pieces are found by moving away from the bomb along the path of travel of the shock wave, since the pieces all move with the blast. They may be deeply embedded in walls (or even people) and difficult to find, but they can be very valuable evidence in court. In addition, pieces of the bomb can be examined to determine more specific information about the bomb itself, such as the chemistry of the components and the amount of energy generated by the explosion.

Bombs come in many shapes and sizes—from letter bombs no bigger than a standard envelope, to large box vans driven onto parking ramps and left to explode. The size of the bomb obviously has an effect on the potential damage it can do, but a well-placed letter bomb can kill just as easily as a truck packed with dynamite.

Using physics to solve crimes takes intelligence and thorough understanding of the principles involved. In most cases, it also requires extensive education.

CHAPTER SEVEN

Focus on Career: Becoming a Forensic Physics Expert

A number of forensic careers make use of a knowledge of physics. These careers are acted out in various realms of crime investigation.

FORENSIC ENGINEER

In many cities, there is a special position in the forensic laboratory called *forensic engineer*. A forensic engineer is a specialist with knowledge and training in either chemistry or physics (or both) and an understanding of their applications in building structures. A forensic engineer with a background in physics might be called on to examine the effect of an explosion on the structure of a wall. Forensic engineers also have an advanced understanding of building codes and standards. A board of their peers in forensic science, as well as the boards of engineers of their particular field of expertise, usually certify them.

In general, forensic engineers are not full-time employees in any but the largest cities. Most forensic engineers, as a circumstance of the lack of work for a forensic scientist with this specific type of expertise, find they must work in other branches of engineering to make ends meet. Of course, this depends on the individual, but in general, the pay for a part-time forensic scientist is not very satisfying.

Some forensic engineers are greatly respected in forensic science, and so are called to be expert witnesses in court cases. In addition, some forensic engineers find work consulting for law firms or insurance companies investigating insurance claims or lawsuits.

FORENSIC PHYSICIST

The path to becoming any sort of forensic expert requires a college education and usually a large amount of on-the-job training. A handful of colleges in the United States provide foren-

A career in forensic science requires several years of college.

sic training at present, but the number is expected to increase as the field grows in popularity. The specific training of a forensic physics expert is heavy in mathematics and science because many of the formulas necessary for an understanding of physics require complicated calculations. Having a solid math background is important for a person interested in forensic physics as a career.

COLLEGE COURSEWORK

For any career in forensic science, a well-rounded four-year college curriculum from an accredited school is recommended.

Some universities offer a specialized degree in forensic science.

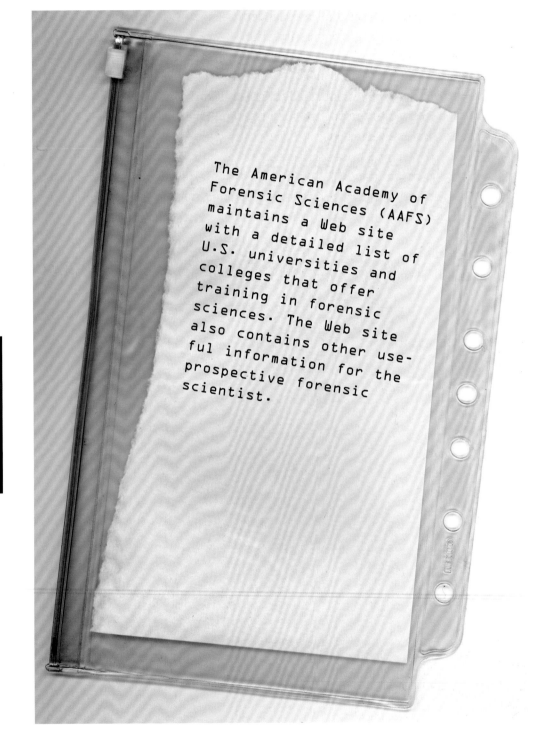

The American Academy of Forensic Sciences (AAFS) maintains a Web site with a detailed list of U.S. universities and colleges that offer training in forensic sciences. The Web site also contains other useful information for the prospective forensic scientist.

Most of these colleges offer degrees in the sciences that give a broad overview of the three major branches of science: biology, chemistry, and physics. Coursework in each of the major sciences exposes students to many of the skills they will need to work in forensic laboratories. The equipment of a forensic laboratory is very expensive and highly specialized. Being comfortable with a wide variety of laboratory equipment is an asset for a prospective forensic scientist.

In addition to the operation of specialized equipment, forensic scientists must learn the proper techniques accepted

Aspiring scientists should spend time in the lab to become familiar with the equipment.

in science laboratories. Knowing how to use a mass spectrometer is not much good if the person does not have the skills necessary to load the samples into it. Learning the basics of bench work in a laboratory is one of the keys to getting started in forensics. The laboratory experiences attached to many college science courses give students ample time to practice these skills.

An individual interested in a bachelor of science degree in physics will most likely be required to take at least two courses in biology and two in chemistry. Some colleges require more, because there is a large amount of overlap between all the sciences, and a good understanding of any one of them requires some knowledge of the others. In addition to biology and chemistry courses, a degree in physics might require several

A preparatory education for a career in forensic science is multidisciplinary.

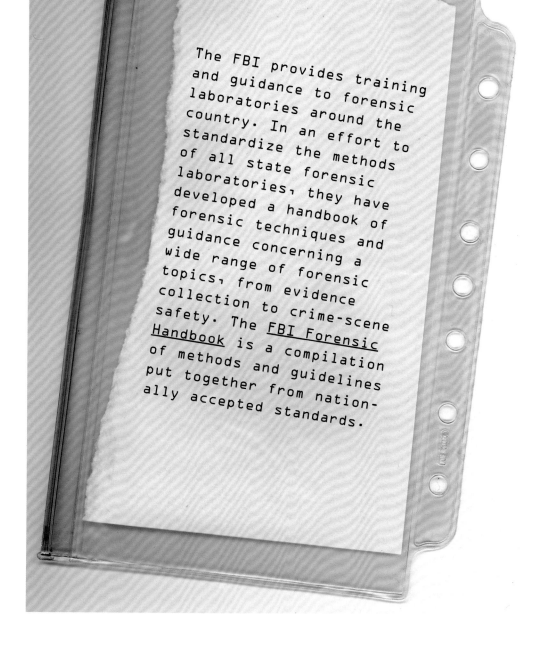

The FBI provides training and guidance to forensic laboratories around the country. In an effort to standardize the methods of all state forensic laboratories, they have developed a handbook of forensic techniques and guidance concerning a wide range of forensic topics, from evidence collection to crime-scene safety. The <u>FBI Forensic Handbook</u> is a compilation of methods and guidelines put together from nation- ally accepted standards.

advanced mathematics courses, such as calculus. Most colleges also require courses in literature and composition, which should not be taken lightly by a student hoping to become a forensic scientist. Much of the daily work of a forensic expert requires extensive reading and writing of peer-reviewed research articles. Staying current in science is important, and the best way to do that is to read.

Forensic scientists often act as expert witnesses in court. In light of this, it is highly recommended that prospective

Time on the job is the best training.

forensic scientists take at least one class in law to introduce them to basic courtroom proceedings and the way the rules of evidence affect their work. Having one's credibility questioned in front of a jury can be stressful for a forensic expert, but understanding the rules can help make it easier.

INTERNSHIPS

Perhaps the best way to find out if a career in forensic science is right for you is to work as an intern for a few months in a forensic laboratory. Most crime laboratories offer internships once or twice a year, so opportunities are available for the right students. Being in the laboratory every day and seeing the operations from the inside can shed light on the way things work there. Internships help students see what their forensics jobs would really be like—and it's usually not how they are presented on television. If a person goes into a career with unrealistic expectations, he may find himself disappointed and presented with the choice of either working at a job he does not love or leaving and risking the financial hardship that comes with changing careers. Sometimes, a lucky student will manage to land a paid internship, though these are rare in forensics because of laboratories' tightly controlled funding. Keep in mind that the internship experience is more valuable than most college classes. It is worth a financial sacrifice to find out if forensic science is the right field for you.

ON-THE-JOB TRAINING

Because forensic physicists are asked to handle such a wide array of work, they must be ready to cope with a wide variety of different situations. No college coursework or laboratory experience can prepare a student for all the problems that can arise in the daily operation of a laboratory. To cope with this, most forensic laboratories hold regular on-the-job training seminars for their employees. In addition to seminars, most forensic laboratories require that newly hired forensic scientists work closely with more experienced staff who are

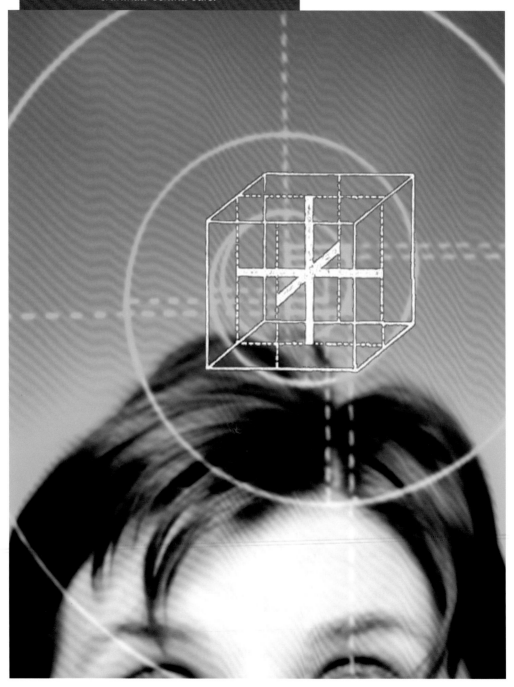

Applying physics to crime-solving helps put criminals behind bars.

qualified experts in their fields. New employees are not allowed to handle evidence alone until they have proven they will not make mistakes that can cost the laboratory money or ruin evidence.

Becoming an expert in forensic physics cannot be achieved in a short period of time. It requires a lot of reading, field experience, and practice, as well as more formal education. With the proper training, however, a knowledge of physics provides important insights into crimes—and these insights can help bring criminals to justice.

Glossary

aerodynamics: The study of objects moving through air.

entomologists: Scientists who study insects.

expending: Using up.

genetics: Characteristics passed on through heredity.

impart: To transmit knowledge or identifying marks.

platelets: Blood particles involved in clotting.

radius: The area within which something can work.

satellite: An offshoot of something larger.

shock wave: A wave of increased heat or pressure that moves outward from a central point of force.

spatter: Small, scattered particles of something, such as blood.

superior vena cava: The vein that carries blood into the right atrium of the heart.

viscosity: The property of a fluid or semifluid that causes it to resist flowing.

Warren Commission: The popular name of the U.S. Commission to Report upon the Assassination of President John F. Kennedy, formed through an executive order by President Lyndon B. Johnson to investigate the assassination of President Kennedy. Members included U.S. Supreme Court Chief Justice Earl Warren and future president Gerald R. Ford, then a representative from Michigan.

Further Reading

Camenson, Bythe. *Opportunities in Forensic Science Careers*. New York: McGraw-Hill, 2001.

Di Maio, Vincent J. M. *Gunshot Wounds: Practical Aspects of Firearms, Ballistics, and Forensic Techniques*, 2nd ed. Boca Raton, Fla.: CRC Press, 1999.

Evans, Colin. *A Question of Evidence: The Casebook of Great Forensic Controversies, From Napoleon to O. J.* Hoboken, N.J.: Wiley, 2002.

Evans, Colin. *The Casebook of Forensic Detection: How Science Solved 100 of the World's Most Baffling Crimes*. Hoboken, N.J.: Wiley, 1998.

Fickett, Wildon. *Detonation: Theory and Experiment*. Mineola, N.Y.: Dover Publications, 2000.

Genge, Ngaire. *The Forensic Casebook: The Science of Crime Scene Investigation*. New York: Ballantine Books, 2002.

Lyle, Douglas P. *Forensics for Dummies*. Hoboken, N.J.: For Dummies, 2004.

Miller, Hugh. *What the Corpse Revealed: Murder and the Science of Forensic Detection*. New York: St. Martin's True Crime Classics, 2000.

Platt, Richard. *Crime Scene: The Ultimate Guide to Forensic Science*. New York: DK Publishing, 2003.

Ramsland, Katherine M. *The Forensic Science of C.S.I.* New York: Berkley Publishing Group, 2001.

Rinker, Robert A. U*nderstanding Firearm Ballistics: Basic to Advanced Ballistics: Simplified, Illustrated, and Explained*, 3rd ed. Corydon, Ind.: Mulberry House Publishing, 1999.

Saferstein, Richard. *Criminalistics: An Introduction to Forensic Science*. Englewood Cliffs, N.J.: Prentice Hall, 2001.

For More Information

Basic Ballistics
members.aye.net/~bspen/ballistics.html

BCSO-Identification Division-Blood Spatter
www.brazoria-county.com/sheriff/id/blood

Blood-Spatter Analysis
www.bergen.org/EST/Year5/EA/Serology2_1.htm

Bloodstain Pattern Analysis
www.bloodspatter.com/BPATutorial.htm

Carpenter's Forensic Science Resources
www.tncrimlaw.com/forensic/f_criminalistics.html

FAQS—NEAFS
www.neafs.org/faqs.htm

Forensic Science, Forensics, and Investigation
www.crimelibrary.com/criminal_mind/forensics

Introduction—FBI Forensic Handbook
www.fbi.gov/hq/lab/handbook/intro.htm#forensic

Reddy's Forensic Home Page
www.forensicpage.com

Wound Ballistics
www.firearmstactical.com/wound.htm

Publisher's note:
The Web sites listed on this page were active at the time of publication. The publisher is not responsible for Web sites that have changed their addresses or discontinued operation since the date of publication. The publisher will review and update the Web-site list upon each reprint.

Index

air resistance 32

ballistic gell 81, 83
ballistics 77, 79–80, 83
blood (analysis and testing) 41, 64
blood (facts and characteristics) 40–41, 43–48, 56, 61
blood evidence 22, 39–42, 49, 51, 54–55, 57–73
blood loss (passive and projected) 49, 51
blood pressure 48, 51
blood spatter 34, 37, 40–42, 44, 46, 51, 53–71, 73, 79, 93
bomb squads 87, 90
bombs 85–93
bullet drop 77, 80
bullet energy 79
bullet path 79–80, 83
bullets 77–83
Bureau of Alcohol, Tobacco, Firearms, and Explosives (ATF) 91

chain of custody 21, 25
chemistry (of explosions) 88, 90
crime-scene reconstruction 59–60

databases 80, 83
Department of Justice 91
DNA 20, 22, 42–43

education and training (requirements for forensic careers) 20, 25, 95–100, 102–103
evidence collection 18, 22, 25
evidence collection unit (ECU) 22
evidence processing 24

FBI Forensic Handbook 101
forensic biologists 18, 22
forensic engineer 95–96
forensic entomology 18, 20
forensic firearms examiner 77–80, 83
forensic physicist 22, 34, 60, 65, 95–97, 100, 102–103

Picture Credits

Artville: p. 40

Benjamin Stewart: pp. 23, 50, 56, 57, 59, 60, 64, 66, 68, 70, 71, 72

Corbis: pp. 79, 80

Corel: p. 87

ImageSource: p. 49

LifeArt: p. 47

MK Bassett-Harvey: p. 67

Photos.com: pp. 13, 15, 16, 18, 20, 24, 28, 30, 33, 35, 36, 42, 44, 54, 61, 62, 76, 82, 88, 90, 92, 96, 97, 99, 100, 102, 104

Whitehousetapes.org: p. 10

To the best knowledge of the publisher, all other images are in the public domain. If any image has been inadvertently uncredited, please notify Harding House Publishing Service, Vestal, New York 13850, so that rectification can be made for future printings.

Biographies

AUTHOR

William Hunter lives in Arcade, New York, with his wife, Miranda, and new baby, Elspeth. He is a high school biology and chemistry teacher in upstate New York. He is a graduate of the State University of New York at Buffalo, earning a master's degree in biology. His interest in forensic science led him to complete elective coursework in the forensic science training program at the University of New York at Buffalo. The author has also been involved in the development and testing of a series of forensic science educational activities, as well as a comprehensive activity for a national science conference.

SERIES CONSULTANTS

Carla Miller Noziglia is Senior Forensic Advisor, Tanzania, East Africa, for the U.S. Department of Justice, International Criminal Investigative Training Assistant Program. A Fellow of the American Academy of Forensic Sciences, Ms. Noziglia is Chair of the Board of Trustees of the Forensic Science Foundation since 2001. Her work has earned her many honors and commendations, including Distinguished Fellow from the American Academy of Forensic Sciences (2003) and the Paul L. Kirk Award from the American Academy of Forensic Sciences Criminalistics Section. Ms. Noziglia's publications include *The Real Crime Lab* (coeditor, 2005), *So You Want to be a Forensic Scientist* (coeditor 2003), and contributions to *Drug Facilitated Sexual Assault* (2001), *Convicted by Juries, Exonerated by Science: Case Studies in the Use of DNA* (1996), and the *Journal of Police Science* (1989). She is on the editorial board of the *Journal for Forensic Identification*.

Jay A. Siegel is Director of the Forensic and Investigative Sciences Program in the School of Science at Indiana University, Purdue University, Indianapolis. Dr. Siegel is a Fellow of the American Academy of Forensic Sciences, and is a member of the Forensic Science Society (England) and the editorial board of the *Journal of Forensic Sciences*. His publications include chapters in *Analytical Methods in Forensic Science* (1991), Forensic Science (2002), and *Forensic Science Handbook, vol. 2*. He is the coauthor of the upcoming college textbook *Fundamentals of Forensic Science*. Dr. Siegel has also appeared as an expert witness in many trials and as a forensic expert on television news programs.